GOOD NEWS FROM DETROIT

SERMONS FOR LIVING THE PRACTICAL CHRISTIAN LIFE

PREACHED FROM A CITY PULPIT

PUBLISHED BY

METROPOLITAN PRESS
8000 WOODWARD AVENUE
DETROIT, MICHIGAN 48202

GOOD NEWS FROM DETROIT
SERMONS FOR LIVING THE PRACTICAL CHRISTIAN LIFE
PREACHED FROM A CITY PULPIT
Copyright © 1998 BY WILLIAM K. QUICK

FIRST PRINTING 1998

All rights reserved.

No part of this work may be reproduced or transmitted in any form or by any means, electronic or mechanical, including photocopying and recording, or by any information storage or retrieval system, except as may be expressly permitted by the 1976 Copyright Act or in writing from the publisher. Requests for permission should be addressed in writing to Dr. William K. Quick, 1941 Wellesley, Detroit, Michigan 48203.

The sermon, "Follow Me", was first published in 1992 by the World Methodist Council, Joe Hale, Editor, in <u>The Sixteenth World Methodist Conference in Singapore</u>, and is used by permission.

"Whoever Finds This - I Love You" *(Mac Davis) Copyright* © 1970, 1972 SCREEN GEMS-EMI MUSIC, INC. All Rights Reserved. Used by Permission.

Scripture quotations, unless otherwise noted, are from the New Revised Standard Version, Copyright 1989, by the Division of Christian Education of the National Council of the Churches of Christ in the USA, and used by permission.

Library of Congress Cataloging-in-Publication Data
QUICK, WILLIAM K. (WILLIAM KELLON), 1933—
Good News From Detroit / William K. Quick. —Rev.

p.   cm.
ISBN: 1-57502-840-9
1. Sermons, American. 2. United Methodist Church (U.S.)—Sermons. 3. Methodist Church—Sermons. I. Title. 4. Detroit: Preachers

Printed in the USA by

3212 East Highway 30 • Kearney, NE 68847 • 1-800-650-7888

*In loving memory
of*

*Stanley Sebastian Kresge
(1900-1985)
and
Dorothy McVittie Kresge
(1901-1988)*

. . . dear friends and devoted servants of Jesus Christ, whose kindness and generosity enriched the lives of many and whose influence continues to live in the memory of many, including this pastor.

"I am crucified with Christ: nevertheless I live; yet not I, but Christ liveth in me: and the life which I now live in the flesh I live by the faith of the Son of God, who loved me, and gave himself for me."

(Gal 2:20 KJV)

Acknowledgments

The publishing of these sermons is the result of the dedication and determination of some persons vitally involved with Metropolitan United Methodist Church in Detroit, a church which I have happily served for twenty-four years.
 John F. Langs, Chairman of the Pastor-Parish Relations Committee from 1955-1995, encouraged and cajoled his Pastor in a desire to see more of the Metropolitan pulpit messages in print. Joseph Beals, M. D., who succeeded John, did likewise.
 Kenneth G. Wigle, a dynamic and devoted leader and trustee of Metropolitan joined the Church in 1908. He has enthusiastically supported the project.

Virginia Conrad, an able secretary and gifted enabler for the entire clergy and lay staff, was originally responsible for transposing and typing sermons. For this volume we chose from among the sermons those most frequently requested by the radio audience.

My wife, Mary, a Diaconal Minister, edited the first collection of sermons, *Signs Of Our Times*, preached on The Protestant Hour and published by Abingdon Press in 1989, and *Take Five*, published in 1996, as well as other publications. She has spent considerable time and effort producing easily readable texts. Her particular gifts of editing, combined with her insight into *"the spoken word"*, has immensely aided the production of this volume of sermons. Without the persistence of Mary this work could not have been completed. I am deeply grateful for her dedication, encouragement and talented expertise.

Metropolitan's radio ministry has touched the hearts of untold thousands through **The City Pulpit**, heard Sunday mornings on WJR in Detroit and on CKLW in Windsor, Ontario, the two most powerful radio stations in the region.

Paul addressed the importance of preaching: *"How then shall they call on him in whom they have not believed? And how shall they believe in him of whom they have not heard? And how shall they hear without a preacher? For faith cometh by hearing and hearing by the Word of God."* Philippians 3:13-14

— William K. Quick

Foreword

In June 6, 1948—as a lad of 15—I experienced my call to the ministry at a District MYF Youth Retreat in Mt. Gilead, North Carolina.

Fifty years later on June 6, 1998 at the Detroit Conference of the United Methodist Church at Adrian College in Adrian, Michigan, my retirement, along with a score of other pastors, was recognized.

Over these fifty years we have experienced a great scepticism about the value of preaching. In the electronic age that asks for the moon—scientifically, socially and financially—there is little patience with a man or woman standing in a box talking about the change God works in the human heart.

Preaching is the event where God's Word comes to the hearer through another person. The proclamation of the Word of God, as Karl Barth, the great Swiss theologian, put it is "Man's language about God in which and through which God, Himself, speaks about Himself." The Word is always greater than the preacher and human proclamation.

One of the great preachers of 20th century America was J. Wallace Hamilton. He often said, "The Church is slow, the world is in a hurry and the preacher is caught between them." Yet, when I despair over the usefulness of a sermon, I remind myself that the Christian Church was launched with a sermon when Peter "stood up to preach" on the day of Pentecost.

Paul addresses the heart of the issue in Romans: *"How then shall they call on Him in whom they have not believed and how shall they believe in him of whom they have not heard? And how shall they hear without a preacher? For faith cometh by hearing and hearing by the Word of God."* [10:14, 17 KJV.]

The primary influence, indeed, the greatest influence in a call to the ministry is God. It is God who raised up Peter and Paul, Augustine and Francis of Assisi, Luther and Wesley. Any ministry should be grounded in an assurance that Almighty God has chosen the minister for the task. Having said that, we still must look to the Church. Only God can make a minister. This, I believe, is true. But God does not choose to make ministers alone. The Church is the Body of Christ and the making of a minister requires that God act upon us within the organic life of the Church. The creation of a called ministry can be helped or hindered by the disobedience of the Church.

Why have some churches produced so many ministers, while others are barren? Why have some preachers a score of Gospel sons and daughters, and others have never known this wonderful experience?

The life of the Church in any generation will determine, to a large extent, whether young men and women choose its service, and the quality of the ministry in any generation will determine how young people regard it. The Church engaged in small affairs and bickerings will not be attractive to young men and women with stars in their eyes. Why should one spend one's life dealing with bitter orthodoxy or irrelevant side issues?

A major change during my fifty years of ministry which began with young students (primarily) offering themselves as candidates is the large percentage of persons entering the ministry as a second career. The average age in some of our Seminaries is somewhere between 38 and 45. While I am grateful for these second-career pastors, I sometimes wonder if the call had not come earlier but was not acknowledged or encouraged by the Church or by parents who wished to see their children in a more lucrative profession. In fact, I have known some young men and women who have felt a call to ministry, and who faced the outspoken opposition of their fathers, or the more subtle lack of enthusiasm of their mothers. Perhaps this is linked to a lessening of faith in Christ and the Church.

Susanna Wesley, who gave birth to 19 children, said to her sons John and Charles, when they told her they were coming to America as missionaries in 1735, "I should be proud to have a hundred sons going as missionaries." Joseph Fort Newton, said his mother would comment, "Listen only to Jesus; accept what He says about God, what He has shown God to be in His life, nothing else, nothing less; test everything by Him—forget the rest."

Let me emphasize—wise parents will not force their children into any profession, including the ministry. Their privilege is to create an atmosphere of love for Christ and the Church and by precept and example indicate their respect for the Christian Church. Having done this the event is in the hands of God.

As I retire fifty years following my call to preach, I am pleased that during these five decades of ministry, over 30 persons have answered the call to preach.

I thank God that in every generation there are those, who like Jesus in his first sermon at Nazareth, can say "The spirit of the Lord is upon me because he has anointed me to preach . . . "

If I had a thousand lives to live, I would want to be a preacher. What a challenge! The calling of a person for the most relevant of all tasks—preaching the Word—is marvelous to consider.

"How can they hear without a preacher?"

—William K. Quick

Table of Contents

Follow Me --- 1

Facing the Challenge of Change --- 8

Why Does Jesus Love Sinners? --- 15

You Are My Friends --- 20

Freedom's Holy Light --- 25

Is Doomsday Ahead? --- 31

The Art of Living 'In Between' --- 36

The Road From Defeat To Victory --- 42

The Power Is In The 'Yes' --- 49

Rejection: Life's Hardest Blow --- 55

Running Life's Race—To Win! --- 60

The Goodness of God --- 65

Shouting Lips, Shallow Commitment --- 69

Good News From A Graveyard --- 74

Four Critical Questions --- 81

FOLLOW ME!

"And He said to them, 'Follow me...'"
Matt:4:19a

The invitation of Jesus Christ to his Church everywhere in the world is—*"Follow me!"* With those two words Jesus began the Christian movement.

Along a pebbled shore of the Sea of Galilee two brothers were mending nets. Their hands are rough and calloused. They smell of fish. Jesus calls Andrew and Peter, "Follow me." [Matthew 4:19a]

He walks along that Lakeshore a little further and two brothers, James and John, are in their boat with their father, Zebedee, mending their nets. They operate that boat in partnership. They are very successful. They've earned the nickname, "The Sons of Thunder." They're always shouting, taunting, rumbling about something. They are ambitious. They've been brought up to believe 'if you want anything—go get it.' Their mother taught them, 'If you want to get on in the world, you have to push.'

Jesus calls James and John, "Follow me." At once, we are told by St. Matthew, they leave the boat and their father and follow Jesus.

Jesus comes upon a man who is a tax collector for the Roman government. He has sold out to the enemy. Among the most unpopular people in any country is the tax collector. This fellow is running his own racket. He has a computer mind. He has counted money all his life. Can you imagine Jesus wanting such a man—a man who had made a god of money—to walk with Him? Matthew left his seat of customs and followed Jesus.

Look at the twelve Disciples Jesus chose—the twelve He invited to "follow me". They were ordinary men. Most of us would not have voted for any one of them. They quarreled. They were jealous of each other. But here they are:

Andrew and Peter, James and John—the Bethsaida Boys working the best money crop of their day—not from the land, but from the sea.

Matthew—the hated tax collector

Thomas—the doubter, the cautious one, demanding proof, taking nothing on faith

Judas—leader of the underground. A zealot. His blood boils every time he sees a Roman soldier occupying his homeland. He dreams of the Messiah who will drive the hated Romans out and restore the Kingdom.

Bartholomew—Thaddeus—Phillip, who also hailed from Bethsaida, and another James (we know him as James the Less) and the Canaanite called Simon.

"FOLLOW ME!" They walked with Jesus. They lived with Jesus. They listened to His sermons. They saw Him perform His miracles. Blind people received their sight. Crippled people threw away their crutches. Dead people were raised to life again.

These dozen men had more influence on the course of human history than any twelve men who ever lived.

Throughout His three-year ministry, wherever he went, Jesus was constantly inviting people to "FOLLOW ME!"

. . . to a rich young ruler: "Go and sell what you have and give to the poor and come and follow me."

. . . to the balking inquirer: "Let the dead bury the dead. You come and follow me."

. . . to all persons in every generation: "If anyone would come after me, you must deny yourself, take up your cross and follow me."

We need to remember some wise, pastoral words from the Convocation on Evangelism in Jerusalem in 1974. Albert Outler said: "An unconverted church cannot convert the world."

Jesus is calling the Church today, "Follow me!" Jesus is asking the Church throughout the world to invite people who are lost, people who are empty, people who are confused, people who are rich in things and poor in soul . . . to *Follow* Him.

Above all the voices clamoring for our attention, all the gods seeking our allegiance, is the one Voice of the one God who says, "Follow me."

The Twelve followed Jesus from along that Galilean shore and countryside through months of teaching and preaching and healing. He sent the twelve out on pilot missions. They weathered the horrors of the cross and the excitement of the Resurrection.

E. Stanley Jones, one of the 20th century's greatest missionaries, reminds us the Disciples had given up everything but themselves. They gave up the fish business; they gave up the tax business; they gave up their families and friends. But it wasn't until they gave themselves up after days of prayer in the Upper Room that the Holy Spirit empowered them to go out and change the world.

The risen Jesus had promised, "You shall receive power when the Holy Spirit is come upon you. And you shall be my witnesses in Jerusalem and in all Judea and in Samaria unto the ends of the earth."

Jesus walked among the people where they were. The shepherdless masses were touched by Jesus and the Twelve. Jesus took to the open road—to the streets—to the common people.

Methodists must never forget how in the 18th century the Church of England lost touch with the common people. There was another

Follow Me

man sent from God whose name was John — John Wesley. Wesley went on the open road, walked the streets of the great population centers of England. He encountered the mobs. He went to the mines. He preached in the fields and the marketplace! Why? Because that was where the people were.

It's again time for Methodists to leave the safe sanctuary of their churches and once more take Christ to the people. The call is no longer, "Come to Church." The call is, "Get out of the Church building and take the Gospel to the people." Within a stone's throw of every church in every city and town in the world are vast numbers of people who have no interest nor conscious concern for Faith.

The challenge of Sir George McLeod, the great Scot preacher—founder of the Iona community off the coast of Scotland, speaks to us where we are:

"I simply argue that the cross be raised again at the center of the Marketplace as well as on the steeple of the church. I am recovering the claim that Jesus was not crucified in a cathedral between two candles, but on a cross between two thieves; on the town garbage heap at a crossroads so cosmopolitan that they had to write His title in Hebrew, Latin and Greek: at the kind of place where cynics talk smut and thieves curse and soldiers gamble. Because that is where He died, and that is what He died about; that is where the church ought to be and what the church should be about."

Brothers and sisters I am grateful for our Sunday Schools, our Youth clubs, our men's and women's groups. But in far too many places the Church has become ingrown, schizophrenic and we talk only to ourselves. We've imbedded ourselves in a silken cocoon of irrelevance.

Jesus said, "Follow me." Mr. Wesley has instructed us: "Offer them Christ." That is our mission still!

The early Church's most renowned missionary, Paul of Tarsus, preached in the most unexpected places all around the Mediterranean world. He preached to the High Priest. He preached to the Sanhedrin. He preached to Governors Felix and Festus. He preached to King Agrippa. He preached to the centurions. He witnessed and preached the Good News on land and on sea.

In the 28th chapter of Acts Paul is in a storm at sea and he witnessed to the sailors. When the ship was wrecked he witnessed to the natives on the island. In a prison cell in Rome he preached to many who came to him. He wrote letters which changed lives.

In a Macedonian prison cell where he was beaten and chained, he seized the opportunity to win a jailer and his family. [Acts 16] The very church he persecuted and sought to destroy *before* his conversion —the church at Antioch [Acts 11]—he served as pastor *after* his conversion. Paul bore witness in unexpected places!

God is still calling us and calls us to witness in the unexpected places, in the tough places. He calls each one of us to be an evangelist. The greatest Methodist lay evangelist in the 20th century, Harry Denman often said, "Either you *are* an evangelist or you *need* an evangelist. You *are* a missionary or you *need* a missionary." God calls us to tell the Good News—to offer Christ—to extend the gracious invitation of Jesus: "Follow Me." But to accept His invitation and to follow Him is but the first step. Go again to the Gospels to discover the next step!

People who follow Jesus are to do the work of the Kingdom. They witness and work with people at the point of their need. We see ordinary people doing the work of God in the world. There is nothing exceptional about any of them. They hold ordinary jobs. They have ordinary talents. Some of them are only names in the record. Whatever they do for Jesus is so ordinary none of the Gospel writers mention it or remember it. They are a very mixed bag of people who have only one thing in common: a desire to follow Christ.

They didn't wait to grow into saints. They had no expectation they'd become potential prophets and martyrs. Jesus asked a group of fisherman, farmers, business men and politicians to follow Him and they'd become "the salt to the earth". They were earning their living in routine occupations of the day—as mixed as any cross-section of humanity—like any twelve persons chosen for jury duty today. They were credulous and skeptical, mystical and practical, bold and timid, optimists and pessimists, right-wing and left-wing.

There wasn't a preacher or a doctor or a lawyer or a general or a senator in the whole lot. But it was these "Twelve" whom Jesus entrusted with the Good News.

The need of the Church today is for the ordinary people to declare the power which God in Christ has brought to the world. "God was in Christ reconciling the world to Himself." (2 Cor. 5:18) Methodists believe faith and good works belong together. While faith is intensely personal, if it is genuine, it issues outwardly in good works.

More and more I fear that the greatest unused power of the Church—its laity—is laid waste. The plight of the Church is not membership but the lack of discipleship. Oh, how the Church needs to make disciples. Mr. George Gallup, a devout Episcopal layman and pollster, tells us that 94% of the people in the United States profess to believe in God. (Remember, even the demons believe . . . and *tremble*.) We don't need any more people in our pagan society in the United States to profess faith in God as much as we need those who profess the Christian Faith to live out their discipleship.

Follow Me

The Gospel has come down to us from those who were called 'Disciples'. The word simply means followers, or students of a particular teacher. From it we get our word 'discipline' — not always an attractive word in our ears, but it's high time we were reminded that from the beginning the followers of Jesus were under a discipline and not just sentimental enthusiasts. Jesus' message today is not simply one of confirming our best instincts but a summons to accept an exacting and costly way of life.

The New Testament was not written to become source material for the Historical method. It was written to be proclaimed the Gospel of God's involvement with the world. To be Christian is to be involved.

The New Testament is a book written *by* disciples of Jesus in order *to make* disciples of Jesus. It is from them that we hear who He is and what following Him really means. One of the writers, St. John, is quite explicit about this. At the end of his book he notes: "Jesus gave a great many other signs in the presence of His disciples which are not recorded in this book. But these have been written so that you may believe that Jesus is Christ, the Son of God, and that in faith you may have life as His disciples."

The Gospels are not fragments of biography collected for the use of scholars, or to satisfy idle curiosity about the character of Jesus. They are stories about Jesus that circulated from the beginning of the Church to elicit faith in Him and to make disciples. And more than once what began as a casual inquiry within the pages of Scripture ended in an awakening and a commitment to the life of vital discipleship.

If you feel, as I do, that being a disciple of Jesus, following His way, reflecting His love to God and one's neighbors, is a task beyond our powers; if you are conscious, as I am, of a constant failure to be a consistent Christian in word and deed; then take comfort from the fact that these first Disciples who gave us the New Testament were very far from ideal followers and failed their Master time after time.

It's an amazing thing that those whose witness launched the Christian Church in the world were themselves faltering, stumbling, confused, and inconsistent people. One of the strongest arguments for the authenticity of their reports in the Gospels is that they pictured themselves as such dumb disciples, misunderstanding, seldom totally loyal, and in the end cowards who deserted the Master in His hour of greatest need. I think that they would be surprised to find themselves depicted in stained glass with halos around their heads drinking in the words of Jesus.

Most of us claim to be disciples of this same Jesus. We have heard the same teaching. We have been told the story of the cross. We have sworn allegiance to the risen Christ. We need to be reminded that one of the teachings of the Faith is that the greatest among us is the servant of all.

On January 19, 1976, the eve of the inauguration of the newly elected American President, Jimmy Carter of Georgia, I was in Washington along with thousands of other supporters of the new President. Mr. Carter, a devout Christian and Sunday School teacher and his family were staying at the Blair House across the street from 1600 Pennsylvania Avenue—his White House address for the next four years. I carried with me a leather-bound copy of the Good News translation of the Bible, a contemporary English translation published by the American Bible Society.

I knew that the new President was a man of the Word. On the flyleaf of that Bible I had inscribed, "He who would be great among you must be servant of all." Jimmy Carter was not returned to the Presidency by the American people. As President he was humiliated by the Iranian captivity of American hostages imprisoned for 444 days. Moments after his successor, Mr. Reagan, became President it was announced that the prisoners were out of Iranian airspace and on their way to freedom. Mr. Carter was on his way back to Plains, Georgia, a failure in the eyes of a majority of his countrymen. Yet, in the ensuing years he has demonstrated what it means to 'follow Jesus'. He has lived out his servanthood to the Master. He teaches Sunday School. He has been a peace-maker between troubled people in troubled nations. He has been a recipient of our World Methodist Peace Award. President and Mrs. Carter have spearheaded a national effort called Habitat for Humanity which seeks to provide housing for homeless and needy people. He has given himself away for others in the name of Jesus Christ.

It is when we give ourselves away that we find ourselves in His Kingdom. In following Jesus remember His admonition to "Deny yourself, take up your cross and follow me."

Let us never forget the work of the Kingdom is always done by ordinary people who have taken up the cross and who have followed Jesus. His work must become our work! To do His work today Christ has no hands but our hands.

That work, I need to remind you, always starts small. Jesus chose twelve—not an army. Not all of the Twelve turned out as He thought. Yet these disciples turned that ancient world upside down. The work of the Kingdom always begins small—with a few people in a few places. Jesus Himself compared it once to a mustard plant which grows from a very small seed into a very large shrub. [Mark 4:30-32] It often begins with little deeds done in small places.

In Alaska there is the village of Unalakleek. A church was

organized and planted in that village. In the church graveyard is a tombstone which marks the final resting place of the first Pastor in that mission. On the tombstone is an epitaph which bears witness to how God can take the total dedication of one person and transform a whole community. That epitaph reads:

Rev. Axel C. Karlson
Born in Sweden, September 15, 1856
Arrived in Unalakleek, 1888
Died January 15, 1910
When he arrived in this village
There was no Christian.
When he died,
There was no heathern.

Axel Karlson began with little deeds in a small outpost frontier village. He spent his life there! The epitaph tells his story.

Every person who reads this will one day have a tombstone with an epitaph. What will it say? Will it bear witness that you were a disciple of Jesus Christ? That you—an ordinary man, an ordinary woman—accepted the Son of God's invitation to "Take up your cross and follow me?"

One of my heroes in the Faith is a man who began his ministry as a Methodist preacher in England. When the Methodist Conference refused to set him free to live out his calling by serving the poor in the East End of London, William Booth and his wife, Catherine, walked out of that Methodist Conference in Liverpool and founded what we know as the Salvation Army. For the remainder of his days, William Booth spent himself in service to the poorest of the poor. Towards the end of his life he lost his eyesight. On his deathbed a reporter from a London newspaper asked his son, Bramwell, if he might visit his father for one last interview.

Bramwell ushered him into his father's sick room and among the questions the reporter asked was, "What is the secret of your life, Mr. Booth?"

Bramwell reported that his father, with tears streaming down the cheeks of that old soldier of the cross replied, "If there is any secret to my life it is **'God had all there was of William Booth.'**

FACING THE CHALLENGE OF CHANGE

*"Forgetting what lies behind
and straining forward
to what lies ahead,
I press on toward the goal . . ."*
Philippians 3:13-14

We have little time remaining in this final decade of the final century of this millennium. Let us concentrate on the first clause of Paul's resolution "Forgetting what lies behind"—the art of letting go, of closing the door behind us and forging ahead with renewed intentions.

Some retrospect is inevitable and desirable. There is a wise use of memory. The Roman poet, Horace, is right: to enjoy the memory of the past is to live twice over. The chief benefit of travel is the storing-up of good memories. It is wonderful, then, to recall the places we have been and the wonders we have seen.

But most lives, like most institutions, suffer from the dead hand of the past which lies heavily upon us. The ghosts of past failures and mistakes haunt us. The memory of wrongs we have done others and wrongs others have done us oppresses us. We drag too much of our past along with us. Its burden increases with the years to the detriment of strong, effective living. A seasoned traveler learns to travel light, unencumbered by excess baggage. For one who would be ever 'straining forward to what lies ahead,' it is imperative to forget what lies behind.

Older people often complain that they are forgetful; their memory is not as reliable as it once was. Did you ever thank God for the power to forget? Consider a single phase of the matter: our tendency to resurrect vanished alternatives, to brood over past choices, inwardly to debate what might have happened had we made our decisions differently.

In Robert Frost's poem, "The Road Not Taken", a traveler tells how he came to a fork in the road and gazing ahead as far as he could see, he made a decision. Looking back, he realized how it had affected all his life thereafter.

> *I shall be telling this with a sigh,*
> *Somewhere ages and ages hence;*
> *Two roads diverged in a wood, and I—*

I took the one less traveled by,
And that has made all the difference.

This mood comes to us all. We feel with Maud Muller that "Of all the sad words of tongue or pen, the saddest of these, 'It might have been.'" The road we *did not* take seems to contain all we sought and failed to find on the road we *did* take.

Paul came to a crossroads at Troas. Recovering from an illness, he discussed with his helpers, Timothy and Silas, where he should go next—to Bithynia or to Macedonia. Having decided on Macedonia, he took a ship across the Aegean to the port of Neapolis, made his way inland to the city of Philippi, gathered a few converts about him and formed them into a church, the first Christian Church in Europe. So it was that the faith was carried from the continent where it arose to the continent from which our ancestors came.

But were there not hours . . . as when he was arrested, beaten, and thrown into jail in Philippi, or when the blase Athenians received his message with yawning indifference, or when he found himself involved in the feuds and dissensions of the cantankerous Church in Corinth, when the word *Bithynia* sounded like music in his ears and he said to himself ruefully, "How different my life would have been had I turned East instead of West at Troas that day?"

Jesus faced a crossroad when a delegation of Greeks came to Jerusalem, seeking him. Should he go with them into a more cultured environment, a potentially wider reach of influence, and there, with abler backing, make his bid to the Greek-speaking world? Or should he stay in little Palestine, among his own countrymen whose leaders were increasingly hostile to him?

As the Cross loomed before him, may there not have been moments . . . as when he knelt in the shadows of Gethsemane and prayed that the cup be taken from him, or when he heard the crowd shouting outside Pilate's judgment hall, "Crucify Him" . . . when the rejected invitation of the Greeks came disturbingly to his mind; "Might I have avoided all this had I gone with them?" It's only to recognize his full and true humanity to suppose there may have been such times.

Let me tell you about a pastor who did so well in his first parish that after seven years, he was called to a much larger church. So firmly rooted in his work there, he declined the tempting offer. Then trouble began. Whenever anything went wrong in his church, whenever he was tired or discouraged, his thoughts turned wistfully toward the rejected opportunity. The other church took on a golden aura in his mind.

Eight years later another invitation came and he accepted. Then, after the excitement of the new venture had subsided, the mood of regret came over him. Why had he left the dear old place, the dear people he knew and loved, who knew and loved him? These backward glances over his shoulder divided and distracted his mind. In his stronger, saner moments, he despised himself for his weakness. But there it was.

And there it is with many of us . . . this proneness to weaken the mind in its executive function by keeping it a court of appeals reviewing old decisions; to revert to yesterday's decision with the futile wish that we could undo it; to daydream fondly of the road we did not take. "Had I accepted the offer I declined, had I gone into another line of work that I considered, had I taken a different kind of education, had I located in another place, had I married a different woman or different man, how much better off might I be?"

This mood is especially likely to assail us at the close of the year when many have the habit of taking an inventory of their lives. On the verge of a new year, a new decade, a new millenium, as we take stock of ourselves, it is a sobering thought that having committed ourselves to a certain course, we have no alternative but to follow it; that there is little but same-ness and repetition ahead, demanding a continuance of the same effort we have been expending.

An outstanding preacher once told me that for thirty years the question uppermost in his mind had been, 'What shall I preach about next?' and so he retired. When a preacher can only see a long procession of Sundays moving toward him—ready or not; when a doctor sees only room after room, ward after ward of tortured bodies appealing for relief; when a businessman sees only a long series of days filled with interviews, appointments, calls, attention to routine detail, neverending problems of personnel; when a teacher thinks of hundreds of children (some yet unborn) who will pass through her class before she's eligible for her pension; when a homemaker reflects on all the beds she must make, meals to plan, prepare and clear away—it seems only human to rebel at the thought that we are stuck on an endless ride on a merry-go-round.

We're tempted to say, "How foolish I was to choose as I did. How much happier I would be had I followed the other road."

It must be conceded that not all choices are wise, that the road we choose is not always the right road, and that sometimes there is valid reason to break away from it and turn what is left of our work-a-day life in another direction.

Phillips Brooks failed as a teacher in Boston's Latin School. Giant that he was, he could not keep order and he was in abject misery because of his humiliating experience. How fortunate not only for him but also for the multitudes whose faith was strengthened by his preaching and whose lives were blest by his radiant, God-illumined personality that, instead of persisting in an uncongenial occupation, he turned to one that gave full scope to his gifts.

Most men never get that chance — that second chance. To change their profession would expose their families to economic hardships while they were preparing for it and getting established in it. So they stick to the work they are in and find most of their satisfactions outside working hours—a less than ideal situation.

But I'm thinking not of the few who have legitimate cause for change, but of the far larger number whose desire for something different comes from a restless or discouraged mood.

To such, it must be said that one reason the road we did not take seems alluring is that we know so little about it. How could you know that your journey would have been more pleasant had you taken the other fork in the road, chosen the other job offered, settled in a different place, married the other man? Had you taken the other road, every subsequent choice would have been different. You do not know where that road would have led. Nothing is so futile as to resurrect vanished alternatives. It leads to self-pity, a trait which will not endear you to those who have to live with you. It leads to envy. Envy is an acid which eats away the soul's peace. It is the only vice I can think of to which no pleasure is attached.

We do well to remind ourselves that, as far as commitment is concerned, the result would have been the same on any road. And all roads are alike in this: we pass through gloom as well as sunshine. There are stretches that are solid and smooth where we make good progress, and there are stretches where our feet sink deep in mire. For every foot of altitude we gain, we must exert ourselves, for whatever the road, climbing means effort . . . breath comes hard and muscles ache.

Furthermore on all roads, when the thrill of adventure passes, and the charm of novelty wears off, the future comes toward us wearing the gray robe of monotony.

To the sentimentalist, to one who has never tried it, the care of small children seems the most enchanting of occupations. A junior executive, whose Junior League wife lived an idyllic existence in their pleasant suburban colonial while he slaved away in his office downtown, was persuaded to mind their three small children one Saturday afternoon while the wife went away for lunch and some shopping with other young mothers. On her return, her frayed and haggard husband presented her with this itemized account: "tied shoe laces 16 times; dried tears, 14 times; blew noses 17 times; served water, 7 times; cautioned children not to cross street, 34 times; children crossed street, 34 times; number of future Saturdays Dad will mind these three children: none!" But that is what child-rearing is all about.

When Charles Eliot was president of Harvard, he said that nine-tenths of his work was as monotonous as the janitors' work: letters to answer, speeches to prepare, a series of people to see, committee meetings to attend, faculty appointments to make. Life is largely made up of repetitive duties and routine tasks. These are not defects of the road we travel. They are the very landscape itself.

Let me say it in all candor as we face a new millennium: the road each of us travels offers life's richest rewards. Duty well done, a clean piece of work held up to God, the realization that we have been able to help where help was needed, a quiet word of appreciation given or received, the respect of our fellow workers, the love and trust of friends: these are life's durable satisfactions.

Whether it is preaching a sermon, singing a solo, performing a surgical operation, teaching math to the vagrant mind of a child, arranging furniture in a living room—the satisfaction depends not on the size of the task but on doing it well.

We don't have to travel a king's highway to live a great life. The dictator may exercise his absolute power and command luxury, but one day will come when a Sadaam Hussein or a Fidel Castro will reap what has been sown.

The common road holds all the essential satisfactions. If we do not find them it is because we are blind—we have eyes but do not see.

How easy it is to play the hero on the road we *did not* take while we fail to live up to the possibilities of the road we are on.

This brings me to my last proposition as we face the year 2000 A.D. People who travel through life complaining about their cramped and thwarted circumstances, are square pegs trying to fit into round holes. My sympathy for them is real. But, by and large, the trouble lies not in the road they are traveling but in themselves and their inability to live above their circumstances.

One of the plays which impressed me most in my drama classes at Randolph-Macon College was J. M. Barrie's "Dear Brutus". The title, of course, comes from Shakespeare: "The fault, dear Brutus, is not in our stars, but in ourselves . . . "

The play is a working out of that theme. Act I introduces us to a group of people at a house party. All are ineffective, dissatisfied, have 'taken the wrong turn,' feel themselves victims of an unjust fate, and want a chance to begin again. In Act II, their host takes them into a magic forest where each gets the second chance longed for, only to find that, though their circumstances have altered and their dreams have come true, they themselves (with a single exception) are the same people as before. In the final act they return to the house, are disenchanted, and are forced to face the bitter truth that the fault is not in their stars but in themselves.

My pastoral assignments have been changed more than once. Always I have brought to the new church and the new task the same limitations, the same temperamental defects, the same imperfect self-discipline. In each of the parishes I have served, I have faced the same problems, dressed a little differently but in essence the same. In each, I have found the same kinds of people: some easy to get along with, some hard to get along with; some a source of inspiration, others a source of exasperation. And always my most difficult problems have been with myself.

For most of us it is not another road we need, it is a renewed self with which to walk the way that lies before us toward a rebirth of patience, courage, determination, faith. This is especially true for those of us who have reached the stage where we tend to slump and let ourselves get bogged down.

Many of the careers on which history loves to linger were wrought out of handicaps well nigh unconquerable.

David Livingston has always inspired me. He educated himself as he tended a loom amid the noise of a textile factory. David Livingston's name is linked to Henry M. Stanley, child of an unwed mother, whose only education was in intolerable working conditions under a brutal taskmaster.

William Carey was a cobbler who became the pioneer missionary to India, an accomplished and versatile linguist and scholar as well as a saint. His immortal words are carved in the tower of the Scarritt-Bennett Center in Nashville: "Attempt Great Things for God; Expect Great Things From God."

John Bunyan was a tinker who, while in Bedford Jail, wrote the greatest allegory of our English language, *Pilgrim's Progress.*

Although blind, John Milton wrote the one great epic of our English tongue, *Paradise Lost.*

Robert Louis Stevenson, while his body was racked by disease, wrote stories, essays and poems which have brought delight to tens of thousands of men, women and children.

Beethoven's deaf ears heard such transporting melodies that, as Wagner said, instrumental music could never go beyond them.

Or consider an Abraham Lincoln, born in the back woods of Kentucky, whose life inspired a country boy from Carolina.

It is such as these who make us impatient with the weak and cowardly folk who blame circumstances for their failure to amount to anything.

Said an old-time humorist who called himself Josh Billings, "In the game of life as in a game of cards, we have to play the hand dealt us. The good player is not the one who always wins but the one who plays a poor hand well."

You and I cannot complain of the deal. The cards were not stacked against us. By undeserved good fortune, our lives are set in a land of opportunity, the envy of the rest of the world. Most of us came into life with a clean heredity behind us, were reared in Christian homes, and were given all the education we were prepared to take.

If we are not making much of ourselves, if we are frittering our lives away, the fault dear people, is ". . . not in our stars, but in ourselves." We have not enough of the classic trinity—grit, grace, and gumption—to put the best that is in us into action, to be the men and women God intended us to be.

In Barrie's play the characters changed their circumstances but not themselves. Most of us cannot greatly change our circumstances, cannot retrace our steps and take the other turning, but we can, if we will, change ourselves.

You say: 'If I had my life to live over, I'd spend more time with my family, try to overcome this or that weakness, make myself more proficient in this or that skill, fill the gaps in my education.'

Well, in the time that remains, why not begin? It's not too late. It never is too late! Are we not all immortal spirits? Doctrines (which we think are so hopelessly old-fashioned we don't say much about them anymore) attempt to express a wonderful truth on which the New Testament insists from its first page to the last: *a person can change, you need not stay as you are!*

Repentance means one turns away from sin. No matter how long you've been sinning, you need not go on.

Conversion means one turns from darkness to light.

Regeneration means one can be born anew even when you are old.

Sanctification means one becomes holy; bringing thought, emotions, imagination and will into harmony with the will of God.

This is the Gospel, the Good News brought into the world by Jesus. If you are in a rut, you need not stay there. If you have a bad disposition, you can change it into a good one. If you have wasted your time, you can begin today to redeem it. Divine resources are available to you. The Power of God is accessible to you—right there on the path on which your feet are set!

"He is able to do far more abundantly than all that we ask or think by His power at work in us" (Ephesians 3:21), and to make us new men and women in Christ Jesus.

Why Does Jesus Love Sinners?

"But law came in, with the result that the trespass multiplied; but where sin increased, grace abounded all the more."
Romans 5:20

The preachers in Jesus' day were the Pharisees, the pure and undefiled men, the men who lived the law, and *knew* what was right and *did* what was right. And into one of those churchmen's home came a "woman of the city", a sinner-woman, a 'street walker'—whose arms had held a multitude of men who were not her husbands. She was a Woodward Avenue woman—a 'lady of the night'—whose very touch was the tawdry hand of the pitiful, paid-for love that answered the human cry of the whole world's lonely life. She came to the feet of Jesus—and upon the feet of the Man who was pure and without sin—she poured her ointment as a gift, washed his feet with her tears, and wiped them with her hair.

And the Pharisee, in whose house she knelt, was angry, and said to himself, *"If he were a Prophet, he would have known who this slut is who washed his feet—for she is a sinner."*

And Jesus turned to his host and said: "Look, Simon—a man had two men who owed him money. One owed him 500 silver pieces and the other owed him 50. They didn't have any money to pay—and he wrote off the debt. Which of the men do you think will love him the most?"

"Well, I suppose the one with the bigger debt."

"You're right," Jesus said. "Do you see this woman? When I came into your house, you didn't give me any water for my feet but she has washed my feet with her tears, and wiped them with her own hair. You didn't kiss me in greeting—but this woman, as long as I've been here, has been kissing my feet. You didn't anoint my head with oil, but she has put her precious ointment on my feet. So, Simon—I say to you—her sins, which are many, are forgiven . . . because she loved, and she loved very much. But the ones who have forgiven very little are the ones who have loved very little. And I am afraid you're one of them. But the sins of this poor, fallen woman are forgiven."

The crowd murmurs. They don't like that. They never do. Who is this fellow who thinks he can forgive sins?

And when he hears them, Jesus looks right at the woman and says: "Your faith has saved you. Go in peace."

And I imagine the air was electric, because preacher-people don't like to be shown up. Good people, proper people, respectable people don't like to think that bad people deserve respect.

It's a tension of the ages. It's a schizophrenic hang-up the Church has always had. Why does Jesus like bad people, and often condemn the good? Why is it sinners are accepted, and the righteous are not?

It is a strange paradox that many good Christians have never quite understood. We have never understood why Christ condemned the Pharisees while seeming almost to condone certain kinds of sin. And we, ourselves, are so often only believers in the law, without ever understanding that Jesus went beyond the law, that he saw into the heart of every single situation of sin, and that the only law through which he looked was the law of love.

I want to tell you today that as I look at the Christian Church in America and at its view of sin, of right and wrong, of good and evil, I am a troubled man. I am troubled at what I myself, have taught. I am troubled at the attitude and spirit I, myself, have shown. I am troubled at the pride and prejudice I have supported, and at the innocence I have condemned. I am troubled at how unloving of the unlovable and how condoning of the cruel I find myself and the Church I love.

I am appalled to be a part of the system. I am furious to discover how forbidding I seem to be which was brought home to me by a recent letter. A woman wrote: "Dr. Quick, I've wanted for a long time to come and talk with you about something troubling, but I did not feel I could. You are so good. Your faith is so great, and mine is so little."

And I wept that I, who like Paul, "as the chief of sinners" and who has preached with passion because it was for the saving of my soul as well as the souls of the people I love, should have appeared so faithful and so good as to be utterly unapproachable to those who were in need; who were sinners in search of another sinner to show them the way to the Saviour. My God! What heresy! What an affront to the whole purpose of preaching! What a shame upon and sham of the shepherd's call to shelter the sheep!

So I ask you to take a new look at sin, and to see how critical it is for the Christian to acknowledge that he or she is a sinner.

First of all, every Christian is a sinner. I am a sinner. You are a sinner. And we fool only ourselves if we say we are not. This has been the historic stance of the greatest Christians from the very beginning. I doubt there was even one of the Master's men who ever forgot whom he really was. Peter knew. John knew. Thomas knew. It's evident in their letters and sermons—in their very preaching of the Gospel.

Paul, the missionary, spoke for them all:

The good that I would do, I do not; but the evil which I would not, that I do . . . I see another law in my members warring against the law of my mind, and bringing me into captivity to the law of sin which is in my members. O wretched man that I am, who shall deliver me from the body of this death? [Romans 7:24]

The Bible says it clearly of us all: "For all have sinned, and fall short of the glory of God." [Romans 3:23] All. Not some. All!

We are all sinners because of a penchant, a tendency, a temptation, a turning toward sin, that is somehow instinctive in every one of us. It is in the atmosphere of the world. It is our heritage as humans. It is congenital; we were born that way. It comes from the free choice of the first man, Adam, who fell from innocence and dragged the whole human race with him. And when we're "doing what comes naturally," we're doing deeds of darkness, turning away from God, and doing, as Paul said, "the very things we do not want to do."

That's just the way it is. We may not want to admit it. We like to think we're good. We spend our energies telling ourselves how good we are. We not only tell ourselves, we try to get others to tell us. We've built up a whole theology of goodness and reward. And no matter what the Bible tells us, we American Christians buy a kind of folk-religion that believes utterly that we are rewarded for our good works, and we'll go to heaven if we're good. We'll make it big in life if we're good. I've had scores of people tell me: "I want to be good in order to go to heaven."

That's a scandalous distortion of what Christianity is all about. It is a complete perversion of what Jesus taught and of what Paul preached. If that were true not a soul in the church nor anyone reading this would make it to heaven because Jesus said, "There is none good but God."

Our first task as Christians is to accept ourselves. It is to be able to say, "Yes, I am a sinner." But the Lord loves me in spite of my sin and I'm not giving up. What am I on my own? I have fumbled so many chances given me by God. But he has chosen me, died for me, loved me, and so I live. And with all my power, I will live for Him and trust in Him and rest my case with Him.

Recognize yourself as a sinner. Look in the mirror and see. There's none good but God. Nobody is. Jesus himself never claimed to be. And Martin Luther went so far as to say: "Sin for all you are worth. God can forgive only a lusty sinner." Luther was saying that at times it's a good thing to have a real sin on your record—a sin big enough that you know you are a sinner because then, there will be no room for pride—which is the biggest sin of all.

Luther goes on to say that good works without faith are "idle, damnable sins!" I believe he meant that the decency of the person who is good just to avoid ruining a reputation is far worse than the indecency of the sinner who shows remorse.

"Lord, be merciful to me, a sinner" is the cry God waits to hear from us. We cannot achieve perfection in this life. And when God commands the impossible of us, he is destroying in us, by our very failure, all illusions of righteousness before he can make us righteous. We must give up all claims to goodness. The way to overcome feelings of guilt is to admit our guilt. Then, there is hope. Then no matter how bad we are, there is a power at work in us that can and will make something out of us.

The Protestant reformer says, "This is wonderful news to believe that salvation lies outside ourselves. I am justified and acceptable to God, although there are in me, sin, unrighteousness and horror of death. Yet, I must look elsewhere and see no sin . . . Before my eyes I see a gulden, or a sword, or a fire, and I must say, 'There is no sword, no fire.' The forgiveness of sins is like this. And the whole effect of it is that the forgiven, unpretentious sinner has vastly more potentialities than the saint."

There is a place for sinners . . . here . . . in this church. This is the place for real sinners. I beg your forgiveness for the times I have made God's children who have come here for healing, feel guilty, feel that the Christian faith is too strenuous, too athletic, too Puritan, and too perfect ever to be attained by them.

J. B. Phillips points out that this is a method almost never used by Jesus. He simply called people to follow him, to walk the high road of life with him. They would soon recognize their sin. And when they did, they would see it, accept it, and be done worrying about it. The folk song sings: "O sinner man, where you goin' to run to? All on that day." When we know we are that sinner man, we will be ready to run to Jesus, for He is our help.

The other side of it: The one thing that keeps the sinner alive, functioning and serving God is that we have a Saviour. As the Epistle to Hebrews has it, we have not for our Saviour a "high priest who can't be touched with the feeling of our infirmities; but was in all points tempted like as we are, yet without sin." [Hebrews 4:15]

Our Saviour knows the sickness of the human heart. He knows about loneliness and love, about temptation and turmoil, about sorrow and suffering. He has been there. And he is far more forgiving than we are ourselves.

He broke through the narrow rule, and saw the universal need — the need for love. And that is what he brought—love to the lost, love to the least, love to the last.

He gave it, instinctively, to those who knew that they were sinners. "Zacchaeus, come down. I'm coming to your house . . . to love you." [Luke 19:2-5]
"Woman, doth no man condemn thee"?
"No man, Lord."
"Neither do I condemn thee. Go, and sin no more." [John 8:10-11] "I come not to call the righteous, but sinners, to repentance." [Matthew 9:13]

Do you know that Jesus was known as a 'loose-liver'—a breaker of the law, an undercutter of tradition and moral values? He let his disciples pick corn on the Sabbath Day, even though it defied the law against Sabbath work, and he said, "The Sabbath was made for man, not man for the Sabbath." [Mark 2:27]

The Pharisees argued about the evils of meat and drink, and Jesus retorted: "It is not what goes into a man's mouth that defiles him, but what comes out . . . for what comes out proceeds from his heart."

Jesus seemed easygoing when it came to those sins of the flesh that we so readily condemn. The sins of the flesh didn't seem to bother Jesus as much as the sins of the Spirit: pride, self-righteousness, and judgment. The self-righteous he puts down every time. But the adulterers, the publicans, the cheaters, went away forgiven. These are the very people today we seem most ready to condemn. Somehow, we are not on Jesus' wave-length. Somehow, we do not see the world through His eyes. Somehow, our moral views are out-of-step with the Saviour's.

What a strange morality we have developed condemning most quickly the things 'bad' people do, but never seeing those cruel casuistries the 'good' people afflict on their neighbors.

Frankly, I ask you to take another look. Begin to see people through different eyes. Dare I say through the eyes of Jesus?

Over my 45 years in the ministry I've counseled a number of pregnant girls and young men in my study and I have seen them change. I've labored and agonized with many couples facing divorce and I've seen them come through on the other side as useful, humble, forgiving, gentle spirits. I think Jesus has something to say. Indeed, we have a Saviour who has compassion for us at the point of our greatest weakness and who is hardest on us at the point of our greatest hardness of heart.

We are sinners. We need a Saviour. And, praise God, we have a Saviour! His name is Jesus!

When we know that our only hope is Jesus Christ, when we acknowledge and confess that we are without hope on our own, then the Saviour's words *"Your faith has saved you; go in peace,"* become the Gospel—the Good News—the *best* news for you and for me!

You Are My Friends

*"A man can have no greater love
than to lay down his life for his friends.
You are my friends."*
John 15:12-15

John was the closest friend Jesus had. A special affection existed between them. As Jesus was dying on the cross he entrusted his mother to John's care. It was because John and Jesus had this close friendship that John remembered and recorded these words of our Lord: *"This is my commandment, that you love one another as I have loved you. Greater love has no man than this, that a man lay down his life for his friends. You are my friends if you do what I command you. No longer do I call you servants, for the servant does not know what his master is doing; but I have called you friends."*

How great is the need to be called 'friend,' and to have someone whom you can call your friend! In the diary of a lonely woman there was this entry: *"Only two phone calls today—one, a wrong number; the other a recorded sales pitch for cemetery lots. If there had really been a person there I think I would have bought one, or maybe two. One for me and one for the friend I never had."* This poignant expression of loneliness carries a feeling of despair.

I guess all of us know something about loneliness. We've been in a strange town by ourselves—not knowing anyone, seeing strange sights, strange faces and being very lonely. Some of us have known loneliness as we've moved to a new city. We've had to start a new life with new neighbors and no friends. Yes, to some degree we all know what it is to be lonely.

Someone has said that *"loneliness is another word for unloved."* It is a desolate empty silence; an unwanted solitude. It's nobody calling your name and nobody caring what your name is. Mac Davis wrote a touching song about loneliness.

> *On a quiet street in the city,
> A little old man walked along
> Shufflin' thru the autumn afternoon.
> And the autumn leaves reminded him
> Another summer's come and gone.
> He had a lonely night ahead waitin' for June.
> Then among the leaves near the orphans' home
> A piece of paper caught his eye.*

And he stooped to pick it up with trembling hands.
As he read the childish writing
The old man began to cry
'Cause the words burned inside him like a brand.
> "Whoever finds this, I love you.
> Whoever finds this, I need you.
> I ain't got no one to talk to ·
> So whoever finds this I love you."

The old man's eyes searched the orphan's home
And came to rest upon a child
With her nose pressed up against the windowpane.
And the old man knew he'd found a friend at last.
So he waved at her and smiled. And they both knew
They'd spend the winter laughin' at the rain.
And they did spend the winter laughing at the rain.
Talkin' thru the trees and exchanging little gifts
They'd made for each other.
The old man would carve toys for the little girl,
And she would draw pictures for him of beautiful ladies
Surrounded by green trees and sunshine,
And they laughed a lot.
But then on the first day of June,
The little girl ran to the fence to show the old man
A picture she'd drawn, but he wasn't there.
And somehow, the little girl knew
He wasn't coming back.
So she went back to her room, took a crayon,
Piece of paper, and wrote
> "Whoever finds this, I love you.
> Whoever finds this, I need you.
> I ain't got no one to talk to
> So whoever finds this I love you."

    There is a sense of desperation about that kind of loneliness where we reach out, but only grab emptiness.

    During the Civil War thousands of appeals for pardon came to President Lincoln from soldiers who had been arrested for violating their duties. Each appeal was usually accompanied by letters of recommendation from important people. One day his secretary put on his desk a single sheet, an appeal from a soldier. Lincoln asked, "Is this all? This man has no friends?"

    "No sir, not one."

    Then said Lincoln, "I will be his friend."

How desperately we need someone to be our friend. There are lonely people in our world who wish for, long for, a friend. This is why the words of Jesus are words to us. For Jesus was not simply speaking to his disciples who were at hand, he was speaking to all the lonely people of the world when he said, "You are my friends."

Jesus offers his friendship and his love telling us that we are not alone. We know that life is fulfilled by our friendships. Someone said that loneliness is hell and friendship is heaven. An English publication offered a prize for the best definition of *'a friend'*. They received thousands of answers and the one they selected as the best was, "A friend is one who understands our silences." You see, a real friend is a person who is in tune with us. A friend feels as we feel and is with us through all things. Walter Winchell wrote: "A real friend is one who walks in when the rest of the world walks out."

We know that our lives are shaped by those who love us, and by those who have refused to love us. I remember when I was in the third grade, I heard many of my friends in class talking about a birthday party they were going to that afternoon. One of the boys in the class had a birthday and had invited some members of the class to the party, but not me. And as they became more excited about the prospect of going to the party, I became more depressed and felt more left out. We need to be included, and to include others in our lives. We need friends. Robert Louis Stevenson once said, *"A friend is a present you give to yourself."*

It was early one morning when Ralph Waldo Emerson woke up with a start; he had a tremendous thought which he immediately wrote down. These were the words, "I awake this morning with devout thanksgiving for my friends, the old and the new." Do you remember the words:

> *Cherish friendships in your breasts*
> *New friends are good but old friends are best.*
> *Make new friends but keep the old.*
> *New friends are silver,*
> *But friends long held are gold.*

A deep affection keeps us heart-to-heart with those we call friends.

A prisoner in a federal penitentiary seemed never to have any visitors. On visiting day he always stayed alone in his cell. Word came to the chaplain so he called in the prisoner. *"Ben, I understand that you never have any visitors. Don't you have any friends?"* And Ben replied, *"Oh sure, I've got a lot of them."* he said, *"But, they are all in here!"* It's always good to have friends close by.

Someone has said, *"A dog is a good friend because his tail wags and not his tongue."* Sometimes we lose our friends by our conversations. I recently read of ten ways to lose friends. Here they are. *First*: monopolize the conversation; *Second*: interrupt the other person in the middle of their point; *Third*: contradict the other person directly so you can show him how wrong he is; *Fourth*: talk about yourself, your achievements, your children, your grandchildren; *Fifth*: don't listen to the other person but regain the conversational initiative as soon as possible; *Sixth*: tell little bits of gossip about another that you have heard; *Seventh*: speak with assured authority on the subject which is the other's special expertise; *Eighth*: go into long and tedious detail on little or unimportant things; *Ninth*: reveal things that were told to you in confidence; *Tenth*: ridicule another's opinions and state your own as authoritative and infallible. That's ten sure ways to discourage friendship.

Paul says we reap what we sow. If you wish to reap friends then you have to sow friendliness. Love begets love, kindness receives kindness in return. And the person who would have friends must himself be friendly.

We need, we must, have friends. "A friend," wrote someone, "is a person with whom you dare to be yourself. You don't have to be on guard with him, you can breathe freely. He understands you. You can weep with him, laugh with him, pray with him. Through and underneath it all, he sees, knows and loves you. A friend is one with whom you dare to be yourself." There is no human happiness, there is no human fulfillment without genuine love and friendships. One woman as she was leaving the house of a friend after a visit said, "I shall come again soon, for I like myself when I am with you." Friends do this for us. They help us to be our best and to like ourselves when we are with them.

Elizabeth Barrett Browning asked Charles Kingsley, the great English Christian, "Tell me the secret of your life that I may make mine beautiful too." Kingsley replied very simply, "I have a friend." Jesus Christ said, 'My friendship is available to you. I don't call you servant, I call you friend.' We can feel the openness of his hand to us, inviting us into His friendship, into His life and into His heart.

Jesus was a friend to the oppressed and outcast. The Pharisees accused Him of being a friend of sinners, and their accusation was correct. For Jesus was a friend of those who needed Him, and he still is. The magnificient strategy of Jesus is this: he refused to have any enemies. Even upon the cross he looked down at those who crucified him and said, "Father, forgive them, for they know not what they do."

There is a power in the love of Christ and the friendship of Christ that enables us to know that we are not alone. For He is with us.

An ancient legend tells of two friends who lived on adjoining farms—one alone and the other with his wife and children. They harvested their grain, and one night the man without a family awoke and thought about his grain piled in his bin. "How good God has been to me," he thought, "but my friend with his family needs more grain than I." So late that night he carried some of his store to his friend's grain bin.

And the other surveying his own harvest, thought: "How much I have to enrich my life! How lonely my friend must be with so little of this world's joys."

So he arose and carried some of his grain and placed it on his friend's stack. And in the morning when they went forth to glean again, each saw his heap of grain undiminished.

The exchange continued each night until one night in the moonlight the friends met, each carrying a basket filled on the way to the other's store house. At the point where they met, the legend says, a temple was built.

Our church is a temple of friendship. It is a place of friendly love and support. It is the place where the friendship of Christ is the inspiration for our friendship with each other. In the spirit of Christ we say to each other, "You are my friend."

I look up at you and I say to you, 'You are my friends.' I am your pastor, true, but you have been my pastor also. More than that, the vast majority have been friends to me. You are my inspiration. You sense when I am discouraged and speak words of love and support that sustain me. Many of you have written notes, encouraged and strengthened me. You've shared your personal joys and experiences which have lifted my spirit. Some of you have prayed when I was so tired I thought I couldn't go on. You are my friends. You are more than just my pastoral responsibility. In the name of Christ who is our friend, you are my friends. Let us find this spiritual friendship in Christ: that support which helps us through our crisis and enables us to live our lives as Christ would have us live, saying to us . . .

"You Are My Friends."

Freedom's Holy Light

*"Blessed is the nation
whose God is the Lord"*
Psalm 33:12

Thomas Paine said during the American Revolution, "These are times that try men's souls." These same words could be said of our times. In these days when so much we prize is at stake, it is crucial for us to remember those who gave us the legacy of freedom.

All our lives we have enjoyed the fruits of freedom. Because many of us don't know the story it is easy to take these freedoms for granted.

The fruits of freedom come from seeds planted by others in the past.

A nation's fate, I believe, is tied to its religious loyalties. How did this magnificent political experiment in freedom, called the United States, get its start? It started in the mind of God. America began its life where the Bible begins its story. The first words of the Bible are these: "In the beginning, God." The words written in English over the first instrument of Government used in this land, *The Mayflower Compact*, were these: "In the name of God, Amen."

God led our forefathers to a continent unspoiled by tyranny. He gave them an immortal dream of government *"of the people, by the people, and for the people."* Who else but God could have guided to these shores those men and women with courage to declare their independence, the wisdom to fashion an all but flawless Constitution, and a passion to establish human rights, equality before the law, freedom of speech and press, universal education, citizen responsibility and government and much, much more?

God's hand moves in history.

It was June 7, 1776 in Philadelphia, the city named for, and dedicated to, brotherly love. Richard Henry Lee of Virginia had proposed to The Continental Congress a resolution affirming that "the united colonies are, and of right ought to be, free and independent states." Normally Lee would have been the one to write the Declaration but he was called home to Virginia due to the illness of his wife. A committee was then appointed to write the Declaration. In this group were Benjamin Franklin, John Adams, Robert Livingston, and Thomas Jefferson.

Curiously, Adams and Franklin were overburdened with their

various duties to the Continental Congress so, the youngest member of the Committee was asked to prepare a first draft of the Declaration. Young Thomas Jefferson composed in eighteen days a document that will live forever in the annals of the history of civilization. Adams and Franklin made minor revisions and the Declaration of Independence was then approved by Congress on July 4, 1776. We have celebrated the 221st anniversary of this preeminent symbol of freedom and of the precious rights it promises for all Americans.

I find it ironic that Jefferson had been appointed to the Congress only a short time before to fill a vacancy caused by a resignation. What is still more unusual is that Jefferson remained a member for only a few months.

How can we account for all these events?

Is it not that the footprints of God are clearly visible in these past events? There is no doubt that God not only took a hand in the affairs of men but also gave to them intellectual and spiritual wisdom. The key men involved in the shaping of our nation's destiny took their fundamental belief in God with the utmost seriousness. Most of them had deep roots in a strong religious heritage.

Perhaps Ben Franklin spoke for most of them as, writing in his last year, he wrote: "I believe in one God, creator of the universe. That he governs it by his Providence. That he ought to be worshipped. That the most acceptable service we render him is doing good to his other children. That the soul of man is immortal."

George Washington expressed it: "I am sure that there was never a people who had more reason to acknowledge a divine interposition in their affairs than those of the United States."

As we look back in our history does it not become apparent that God has been our protector? From the dark days of the Revolution, when a handful of people won their freedom from a world empire, let us move forward in history some fifty years.

In the mid-1830s a young man got on a flatboat in Central Illinois with a load of pigs that he and a friend were taking to market downriver. They floated the flatboat down the Sangamon River, into the Illinois, down the Illinois into the Mississippi, and down the Mississippi to New Orleans. Mind you, it was just one young man, with a friend, on one flatboat loaded with pigs. There was nothing imposing about the young man, or his friend, or the pigs, but this combination of small details were the seeds that spelled the beginning of the end of one of the greatest sins in America—slavery. The young man who witnessed the slave market in New Orleans was changed forever. His name was Abraham Lincoln.

Lincoln was the only President in the history of the Republic who never joined a church. But if it is true that a person's knowledge of the Scriptures is revealed in one's ability to translate them into contemporary experience and bring them to bear so that they clarify and reinforce life, then Lincoln may have been our most spiritual President.

The battle at Gettysburg in 1863 took place at a critical turning point of the Civil War. At a memorial service a short while later, President Lincoln spoke for two minutes words that have become almost immortal. I quote from the last few lines of his Gettysburg address:

"It is for us, the living rather to be dedicated here to the unfinished work which they who fought here have thus far so nobly advanced. It is for us to be here dedicated to the great task remaining before us; that from these honored dead we take increased devotion to that cause for which they gave the last full measure of devotion; that we here highly resolve that these dead shall not have died in vain; that this nation, **under God**, *shall have a new birth of freedom; and that government of the people, by the people, and for the people, shall not perish from the earth."*

When President Lincoln said: "This nation, under God, shall have a new birth of freedom," he was not trying to be rhetorical. It was not a religious gesture, a tipping of his hat to the Almighty. It illustrated his belief in the origin and meaning of life, namely that it was conceived by God, and that to find fulfillment it must be lived under God. He was saying that life is not meaningless, that the universe is not like a ship without a rudder. He was saying that the primary fact about a human being is one's relationship to one's Creator.

Two years after Lincoln's Gettysburg address, he was shot by John Wilkes Booth in the Ford Theater in Washington.

As Lincoln's body was being taken from Washington to Springfield, Illinois, it passed through Albany, New York. There, as the coffin was being carried through the streets, it was reported that a Negro woman lifted her little son as far as she could above the heads of the crowd and was heard to say, "Take a long look, son. He died for you."

Americans must never forget that the seeds of freedom are costly seeds—seeds bought with human blood, toil, and tears, bought with lives of those who sacrificed and died for their dedication to the sacred ideal that in the eyes of God all men are equal and endowed with certain inalienable rights.

Americans should never forget the crimson snow at Valley Forge, the slaughter during our own Civil War, the rows of crosses in Flanders Field, bodies buried in watery graves in the USS Arizona at Pearl Harbor, the bloody sands of Anzio, Normandy and Iwo Jima, Pork Chop

Hill in Korea—the place where GI X—the millionth GI to die in the cause of freedom in our country's history—was felled, and in the jungles of Vietnam.

Freedom is a spiritual thing.

Harry Emerson Fosdick said: "The deep fountains of freedom are within the soul." St. Paul said, "Where the Spirit of the Lord is, there is liberty."

But freedom means responsibility. It has long been recognized that liberty without responsibility quickly becomes license.

The author of I Peter wrote to the first century church, *"Live as free men, yet without using your freedom as a pretext for evil, but live as servants of God. Honor all men."*

We are called to plant seeds of a sturdy sense of personal and social responsibility in each generation if we are are to become responsible, contributing citizens in our free society. Freedom is a two-way street. Implied in each 'inalienable right' of democracy is an **'inevitable responsibility.'** Givers and takers of freedom are mutually dependent.

Among the responsibilities of freedom is empathy. Taken from the vocabulary of modern psychology, empathy means entering into an understanding of the feelings of others.

There is room here for us to exercise our creative imaginations. Stop and ask yourself: "How would I feel about this situation or that problem if I were a member of *this* minority group?'

In the glorious but confusing conglomeration of cultural backgrounds and ethnic differences which we call American life, how important that we learn to practice empathy concerning our neighbors! This is the oil that lubricates the social machinery of an uncoerced society.

Moses Lieb, an Hasidic Rabbi, prescribed to his disciples:

"I learned how we must truly love our neighbors from overhearing a conversation between two villagers. The first said, 'Tell me, friend Ivan, do you love me?'

The second: 'I love you deeply.'

The first: 'Do you know, my friend, what gives me pain?'

The second, 'Pray, how can I know what gives you pain?'

The first, 'If you do not know what gives me pain, how can you say that you truly love me?'

"Understand then, my sons, to **love**, to **truly** love, means to know what brings pain to your brother or sister."

It is not easy to practice empathy because our world is so filled with anxieties which focus self on the self. But because of the anxieties, empathy becomes all the more essential. For many of our anxieties arise from interpersonal friction—friction that can be reduced only by true tolerance. Such tolerance can be derived only from understanding the feelings of others.

The Carpenter of Galilee, with profound insight into the human situation, said, "If you continue in my Word, You are truly my disciples and you shall know the truth and the truth shall make you free." [John 8: 31-32]

Do you remember Jesus' parable of the Sower?—the man who went out to sow seeds. Recall that some seed was eaten by the birds, some choked by thistles, some scorched by the sun. Some seed fell on good soil and brought forth fruit—some hundredfold, some sixty, some thirty. [Matt. 13:3-8] All of this is inevitable when anyone goes forth to sow seeds.

I love the old story I first heard in my childhood—the story of Johnny Appleseed. Do you remember it? Johnny Appleseed believed that as the pioneer settlers moved West they needed fruit. So he did something about it. Nobody knows how many hundreds of miles he tramped through the wilderness with a bag of apple seeds. He carried his Bible. Most people don't know his real name was Rev. John Chapman. At each clearing, we are told, he planted his seeds—not only apple seeds, but seeds of religious faith.

In a sense Johnny Appleseed is a symbol of what one person can do for freedom. As Dr. Elton Trueblood put the matter 'A man has made at least a start on discovering the meaning of human life when he plants shade trees under which he knows full well he will never sit.' Johnny Appleseed was sowing for the future.

Leo Buscaglia, that marvelous professor of love and life, wrote, "Don't spend your precious time asking, 'Why isn't the world a better place?' It will only be time wasted. The question to ask is, "How can I make it better?' To that question there is an answer. Finding that answer is your job and mine.

In 1922, just five years after the Communists came to power in Russia, the Bolsheviks had a parade in Moscow in which they carried a stuffed figure labeled, "Almighty God." At the end of the parade they burned God in effigy. That was the smart thing for them to do. If one intends to kill liberty, one had better get rid of God first. For as long as men and women believe that God is the author of their rights and liberties, they will resist the efforts of tyrants.

When, as a nation, we employ phrases such as, "In God we trust" or "This nation, under God", we are recognizing God as the supreme sovereign of our country. There is no room for totalitarian ideals in this nation. For us it is the never-to-be-forgotten words of the Psalmist as he spoke for all ages: "Blessed is the nation whose God is the Lord, and the people whom He has chosen as His heritage."

What takes place when we lose God?

T.S. Eliot, in his classic poem, "Choruses From The Rock," prophesies what happens to a nation that forgets its spiritual values and turns its back on its Creator. He pictures the desolation where the inhabitants have vanished and nothing but weed and rubble remain:

> *"And the wind shall say: Here were decent, godless people:*
> *Their only monument the asphalt road*
> *And a thousand lost golf balls."*

I appreciate our country, as I'm sure you do. But, I worry. I worry about the great unknown in the 21st century, about what lies beyond this millenium—fast coming to a close. I worry about our character, our focus, our sense of stewardship. I am concerned about our lack of a sense of history. I am troubled about our values.

Are we truly grateful for freedom's holy light—this heritage of faith—a heritage which is ours because of the seeds planted by brave men and women in years gone by? How can we hope to repay them for their sacrifice unless we **sow well** the seeds of faith and freedom for the generations yet to be?

We need to recall—and to be thankful—on occasions other than the patriotic observances like Independence Day. The Day is more than fireworks, outdoor barbecues, parades and frolics. The day is an occasion for celebrating the brave step into the unknown that our forefathers dared to take in the name of freedom.

As often as possible, we need to think about and pray for our country and its leaders; to see the challenges and responsibilities that are ours in protecting its rights, and to know in the stillness of the moment that our whole way of life in America is rooted in the fundamental belief that God is our Lord. "Blessed is the nation whose God is the Lord" for this is freedom's holy light.

PRAYER:

Father of all liberties, forgive us for those times when we have honored freedom with our lips—and denied it with our lives. Grant us new insights concerning your truth which alone can set us free. Help those living in places of oppression to seek and to keep the light of freedom burning in their souls. Use us, O Lord, to sow those seeds from which true freedom may flower that your kingdom of justice and love may come on earth—as it is in Heaven. In Jesus name. Amen.

"Is Doomsday Ahead?"

*"Heaven and earth will pass away,
but my words will not pass away.
Beware, keep alert; for you do not know
when the time will come."*
Mark 13:31

Our 40th President, Ronald Reagan, like millions of Americans, is now a victim of Alzheimers. During the first year of his presidency, a Global 2000 Report was placed on his desk. It soberly projected that in the year 2000 there would be *"three persons on earth for every two in 1975, the number of poor will increase, there will be fewer resources, one-half of the world's oil supplies will be gone forever, the per capita water will decline by 35% and the per capita stock of wood would be 47% lower that in 1978. The world will be more vulnerable both to natural disaster and to disruption from human causes."* The study concluded, *"The time for action to prevent this outcome is running out, and unless nations collectively and individually take bold, imaginative steps toward improved social and economic conditions, better management of resources and protection of environment, the world may expect a very troubled entry into the 21st century."*

Has the countdown begun? Is doomsday ahead? Are we living in the last chapter of world history? The answer heard from several quarters is *yes*. In contemporary times it may have begun with Hal Lindsey's predicted Armageddon, *The Late Great Planet Earth*. Listen to some of the radio and television preachers and you hear the same prediction: *'The end of the world is around the corner. We are living in the last days.'*

How should we respond to all this talk of imminent disaster? We are told that enough nuclear weapons remain in the arsenals of some nations to destroy the world and leave nothing but cockroaches to inhcrit the earth. One of the greatest military leaders of the 20th century, General Omar Bradley, said, "Ours is a world of nuclear giants and ethical infants . . . we know more about killing than we know about living."

Given our present unstable political and social conditions, the weapons of biological and chemical warfare many believe under the control of Iraq's Saddam Hussein, is there an increasing probability that some megalomaniac might press a button unleashing chaos upon the world's population? The answer has to be, "Yes, we may well be living in the last days."

More than ever we need to view the march of human events in Biblical perspective if we would see "beyond the shadows of earth the light of eternity." In apocalyptic writings, the scenario goes something like this: When evil triumphs and there is no hope for humankind, deliverance comes swiftly, dramatically, finally. Satan is overthrown, the righteous triumph, and a new age is begun under God's own rule in which the righteous are blessed forever.

I think it's time to think apocalyptically—to ask what is God's will for our world? What is God's plan, for those who believe He has revealed himself supremely in the life, death and resurrection of Jesus Christ?

When we examine the apocalyptic writings: Daniel in the Old Testament, the Revelation of St. John in the New Testament, as well as the apocalyptic strains in the Gospel, some themes emerge that we need to keep in mind in times of crisis.

There will be tribulation! Not even the Saints are excluded from 'wars and rumors of wars.' During His last visit to Jerusalem, Jesus emerged with His disciples from the Temple. "Look, teacher," one of them exclaims: "What wonderful stones and what wonderful buildings!" Jesus replied, "Do you see these buildings? There will not be left here one stone upon another, that will not be thrown down." [Mark 13:1-2] Then follows in the thirteenth chapter of Mark those terrible predictions of what must take place as the end approaches. His predictions turned out to be amazingly accurate. He prophesied wars, and the dreaded Parthians were in fact pressing in on the Roman frontiers. He prophesied earthquakes which devastated Asia Minor. Vesuvius erupted, burying Pompeii in lava. He prophesied famines, and there was famine in Rome in the days of Claudius. It was in fact such a time of terror that when Tacitus began his *histories* he said that everything happening seemed to prove that the gods were seeking, not salvation, but vengeance on the Roman Empire.

As we approach the end of the 20th century we've heard more and more about famines, major ecological dislocations, and the disasters many believe were caused by *El Nino*. It is folly for us to think that we can escape because we see America as a 'Christian' nation and having military and weaponry superiority. The people of ancient Judah thought they were specially blest and protected by Divine Providence. Dare we believe that we have an inherent right of continued and uninterrupted possibilities of growth, prosperity and consumption? Do we seriously believe that God loves us more than the rest of the world?

As we face a possible conflict with Iraq do we believe that our military might would protect us and the free world? Are we not already discovering that the more power we possess the more insecure we feel? No amount of military hardware can compensate for the decline in moral and political prestige plaguing our nation. Yes, in the world we will have tribulation!

What about false prophets? At the same time we must beware of those who presume to know too much: the doomsayers who love the sensational, whose followers are ready to believe anything the latest prophesy-pushers create. There's a well-known radio and TV preacher who claims that 90% of all Biblical prophesy pertains to our day, right now. To claim that the Biblical writers had the last decade of the 20th century in mind and they were addressing their words specifically, if not exclusively to us, is gross misinterpretation.

Do we not remember the Reverend Sun Myung Moon who claims that Christ will come from Korea, the New Israel, marry, have perfect children and set things right again? Prophet Moon says that Jesus may not come in the clouds at all; He could just as easily come from Korea in a business suit. I notice, coincidentally, that Rev. Moon habitually wears a blue business suit and a red tie. We haven't heard much of him the past few months during the latest financial crisis in Korea.

The greatest fallacy is to calendar Doomsday: attempting to put a date on when the end of the world will come. This leads to controversy as the predicted dates come and go as they have for centuries.

Jesus clearly avoided setting a date and we would do well to follow His advice: "An evil and adulterous generation seeks a sign." [Matt. 12:34] When He spoke of impending disaster that would destroy the Jewish nation and bring this present world to an end, His disciples asked, "Tell us, when will this be?" He went on to describe vividly what the end would be like, but was careful to add a sentence that is often conveniently overlooked: "But of that day or that hour no one knows, not even the angels in heaven, nor the Son, but only the Father." [Mark 13: 4 & 32]

Christians, not knowing the day or the hour, have an obligation, a moral responsibility to live expectantly, hopefully. This means working seriously to make this world a better place in which to live.

Martin Luther was asked one time what he would do if he knew the world would end tomorrow. He replied, *"I would plant an apple tree."* To do something beautiful and lasting in a world that is perishing is an important stance to take.

There is a hospital in a suburb of Columbus that was built by a Seventh Day Adventist physician. The Seventh Day Adventists devoutly believe that Christ is coming soon. That being true, one may ask why the Adventists have built some rather substantial and permanent medical facilities instead of temporary shelters, not only in Ohio but around the world. They want these facilities to last and in my judgment, that is not a contradiction. The end could come tomorrow, before sunset, but there's no need sky-watching for signs of the end. Like the Adventists we should plan to continue a ministry of healing and preaching and teaching until He comes.

There is so much misery in our world, so much evil. This is not a time to sit down in idle resignation. We need to make our voice heard, our life count.

There is an old hymn by Maltbie Babcock whose words are a ringing call to action:

> Be strong! We are not here to play, to dream, to drift;
> We have hard work to do, and loads to lift;
> Shun not the struggle; face it;
> 'Tis God's gift. Be strong, Be strong!
> Be strong! Say not the day's are evil, Who's to blame?
> And fold the hands and acquiesce—O shame,
> Stand up, speak out, and bravely, in God's name,
> Be strong! Be strong!

Awkward words but good counsel! Humanity—the community of nations—the whole human family needs to stand together in these difficult times.

Let me tell you a true story and ask you to consider it a parable. Almost a quarter century ago now, during this time of the year, a lovely little child living in a small town in Wisconsin strayed away from her home. It was a bitter, cold winter day. Her mother sounded the alarm that she was missing. Neighbors and friends bundled up and began to look for the lost child. Individually, they combed the woods; walked alongside and across the frozen lakes; trudged through the fields but they could not find her. Then, as night began to fall, one man suggested, *"Why don't we join hands and stand together instead of going separately?"* In this way they discovered the little girl, her body frozen and dead. In the hush of that awful emotional moment, someone sobbed as if to himself, *"Why, oh why, didn't we join hands sooner?"* The pathos of that moment of discovery! We need to relate it to life today in our world. We need to relate it to our church: *"I'm going your way so let's go hand in hand. You help me and I'll help you. Let us help one another while we may."* Can we think of any attitude other than this, any hope higher than this, any possibility more promising than this for our church, for our nation, for our world?

Finally, remember above all else, that though the cause of evil prosper, God is the Lord of history and our lives ultimately are safe in His hands.

In Colonial Williamsburg, Virginia is located the second oldest college in America: *William & Mary College*. Its famous *Old Main* building was designed by one of the Western world's greatest architects, Sir Christopher Wren (who designed St. Paul's Cathedral in London). *Old Main* always symbolizes hope. In 1881 the College of William and Mary closed its doors. They remained shut for nearly seven years. The battles of the Civil War had been fought up and down the Eastern Seaboard and had left the college in ruins. Although it struggled to keep going during the bitter time of Reconstruction following the Civil War, it was finally forced to close by financial catastrophe. Yet this is the story. Every morning during those seven barren years President Ewell rang the chapel bell. There were no students. The faculty had disappeared. Rain seeped through the leaky roofs of those old and now desolate buildings. But every morning President Ewell still rang the chapel bell. It was an act of faith, an affirmation that the powers of darkness do not have the final word.

Some of you may be thinking that's a bit sentimental. Are you suggesting that in the end we're going to get off the hook and everything will turn our all right? No, I don't mean that at all. While all's not right with the world, *God is still in His heaven.* He is still in charge, I believe, of this old earth. His Kingdom is forever.

In the apocalypse of St. John, which we call *Revelation*, there are wars of cosmic proportions. All the powers of Satan are arrayed against the hosts of God. Horrible plagues are unleashed; war, famine, death, conquest—the four horsemen of the apocalypse—stalk the earth. One-third of the human race is wiped out at one time. There is no escape, no hope, no relief.

Then, in the midst of all the carnage, an angel blows a trumpet and from the heavens are heard a great affirmation, *"The Kingdom of this world has become the Kingdom of our Lord and of His Christ, and He shall reign forever and ever."* [Revelation 11:15]

Not "*will* become . . . *has* become." Though Satan still stalks the earth and further calamities too horrible to contemplate lie in store, the ultimate victory of Christ is assured. Therefore, the Christians of the Middle East—of Iraq, of Iran, of Israel, of Turkey, of Asia Minor, threatened by persecution and death—as well as Christians in the United States and around the world—can take heart.

Is Doomsday ahead? When will the world end? In the year 2000? How will it happen? *"No one knows, not even the angels in heaven, nor the Son, but only the Father,"* said Jesus. [Mark 13:32]

And this we can devoutly believe and stalwartly affirm: "Jesus Christ is King of Kings and Lord of Lords. And He shall reign forever and ever. Hallelujah! Hallelujah! Hallelujah! **AMEN.**

The Art of Living In Between

"Then all the congregation raised a loud cry, and the people wept that night. And all the Israelites complained against Moses and Aaron; the whole congregation said to them, 'Would that we had died in the land of Egypt or would that we had died in this wilderness' . . . Let us choose a captain and go back to Egypt."

Numbers 14: 1-2, 4

The Detroit police were called one day by someone who reported a man climbing a tower of the Ambassador Bridge which connects the Motor City with Windsor, Ontario. They assumed, of course, that he was planning to jump to his death, and great was their relief when they found that he was only doing it on a dare and they were able to persuade him to come down.

A similar incident on the George Washington Bridge in New York City was reported a number of years ago, except there the man was planning to commit suicide and nothing the police could say would dissuade him. They contacted a priest to talk to him, but he failed to change the fellow's mind. An onlooker volunteered to climb up and talk with him. Since there was nothing to lose by accepting the suggestion, the police let him climb through the girders. After a few minutes the two came down together.

When the press asked the volunteer how he had done it, he responded, "I told the man that I, too, had once thought of jumping off a bridge. I told him about my own boy who was born with a serious heart defect. What agony it was for me to watch him grow yet not be able to play with and do the things that other kids do, and never know when that 'bum ticker' would quit altogether. When doctors perfected 'open heart' surgery, my boy went to the Mayo Clinic in Rochester to have an operation hoping it might work." Then he closed by saying, "I felt for the guy. He's got trouble. I've had trouble, too. But a man's got to stay on top of it."

When the story was printed, one reporter commented: "Life is all in the fearful hoping, sorrows and joys and 'maybes' *in between.*"

That rings true, doesn't it? That is where we all have to live most of the time, *in between.* In between success and failure, enthusiasm and boredom, hope and despair, sunshine and rain, in between things the way we would like them to be and the way they are. In international affairs we live between peace and war; in energy

we are caught between plenty and want, in management between profit and loss. "Life is all in the fearful hoping, sorrows, joys and maybes in between." For today is ever between yesterday and tomorrow.
They've been working on the freeway close to our house on recent weekends. (Aren't they always? Around here it is said:"Michigan has two seasons: Winter and Road Repair") Sometimes it is open to traffic both ways; sometimes it is closed for south-bound traffic. Sometimes it is closed on Friday nights; sometimes it closes on Saturday morning. Sometimes I forget and I have to go a long way around.
Which is, I think, a parable of life . . . full of frustrations, detours, delays, unpredictabilities. We always want to go by an easy and direct route, but we often have to travel the slow and indirect way, through trial and error and uncertainty.
The late Charles A. Beard, famous American historian, used to preach what he called the "Calamity theory of progress." He pointed out that we seldom advance by deliberate planning. Thousands of people are killed at grade crossings before we devise signal systems or grade separations. Airplanes collide in mid-air before we perfect air control techniques. Nuclear plants go awry before we give full consideration to all their hazards.
We befoul the air and pollute the rivers before we learn the limits of the biosphere. We live most of our days in between the way things are and the way they ought to be.
The question is, how are we to live with the disappointments and frustrations and delays and side-tracks of it all.
The first thing I want to mention is that we can only do it by keeping our poise. One cannot live well in the in-between by over-reacting, giving in to blind anger, yielding to hysteria, or losing one's nerve.
Read from the Bible a part of the story of the Hebrews' trek from slavery to freedom. If you read the whole story at one setting, one of the things that appears is that no small part of Moses leadership was in the way he was able to keep his head when all about him were losing theirs.
Just about the time they ran into an unanticipated delay or detour or difficulty someone would stir up trouble in one way or another; jealousy reared its head [Num. 12:1] . . . When the food ran short they longed nostalgically for the ". . . fish we ate in Egypt, the cucumbers, the melons, the leeks, the onions, and the garlic". [Num. 11:4] When they first heard about Canaanites they were ready to quit on the spot.
"All the people that we saw . . . are men of great stature . . . and we seemed to ourselves like grasshoppers. Then all the congregation raised a loud cry . . . And all the people of Israel

murmured against Moses and Aaron; the whole congregation said to them, 'Would that we had died in the land of Egypt. Or would that we had died in this wilderness. Why does the Lord bring us into this land, to fall by the sword? Our wives and our little ones will become a prey, would it not be better for us to go back to Egypt?'" [Num. 13:28-14:3]

So with many of us. We lose our poise, our cool, and let the fears, the bewilderment, the frustrations of living in between get the best of us. We yield to the hysteria peddlers who trade on our anxieties.

The second thing I want to mention in dealing with our disappointments, frustrations and delays is to count our blessings.

To be in between, as a general rule, is to be better off than where we were. We may be in between slavery and the Promised Land, but that is a lot better than being back in slavery. And for all the bewilderment and confusion and frustration of our own time I would say that the same is true.

I for one, have no desire to go back to those 'quieter' days for which some long nostalgically. Those good old days in race relations when no one mentioned or did much about shocking injustices and second class citizenship. Those good old days when young people simply went off to war without raising any embarrassing questions; those good old days when a manufacturer wasn't responsible for a defective product and an industry didn't have to fool with environmental impact statements.

Tami Hogan was a nine-year old girl. She was described by those who knew her as a shy but thoughtful little girl. She had leukemia; she knew it, but neither the doctors nor her parents ever fully spelled out for her all that it meant. But she knew something was wrong. She didn't have the energy and couldn't do the things that other kids her age did. She once told her teacher that she ". . . wished she could have just one day when she didn't feel sick."

After she died, her parents found a free verse poem. It was written in crayon and Tami had made a drawing to go with it:

> *Thank you Lord,*
> *For letting me be alive today.*
> *I like to try to help in many ways.*
> *Thank you for my family.*
> *We do live quite happily.*
> *We always play together.*
> *Oh, thank you for the sunshine weather,*
> *It's just wonderful to be alive!*

Most of us have wasted more years than Tami had on this earth. But none of us is going to learn to handle our frustrations and

disappointments better than she. Count your blessings!
 In the third place, when it comes to living 'in between' yesterday and tomorrow, the way things are and the way they ought to be, let us look to God to help us. In the Old Testament story of the children of Israel fleeing Pharoah, we had a glimpse of Moses and the Hebrews in between Egypt and the Promised Land. Geographically they were at Kadesh in the northern part of the Sinai peninsula. They had been there a long time, perhaps a generation or two. They had gotten there pretty directly after leaving Egypt, but every effort to break away from that oasis had been frustrated. They thought first to go directly north . . . that was the short and obvious way to go, but they had been turned back by the Canaanites. Then they thought to try another way, around the southern and eastern side of the Dead Sea. There was a trade route called the Kings Highway. It was a natural but the King of Edom wouldn't let them use it, even though they promised to cause no harm and offered to pay for any inadvertent damages. So they had to try still another longer and more difficult way. But, to their surprise, they discovered (and later generations affirmed) that they hadn't had to do it alone . . . God somehow had been with them.
 That is what the faithful always find.
 Jesus taught that what could be observed of humanity at its best can be assumed of God . . . and we have a right to believe that there is a Commander-in-Chief who not only understands the journey but who shows us where we are and what our duty is and promises that the job, no matter what the frustrations, can be done.
 I had the unusual opportunity once to sit next to Tom Sullivan at an event at the Renaissance Center. Who is Tom Sullivan, you ask?
 Tom Sullivan is a blind pianist-singer. Of himself, he says: "Early in life I felt like I had been cheated. Mom and Dad built a fence around our back yard in Connecticut because they wanted to protect their handicapped boy.
 "They thought of it as a handicap; I thought of it as an inconvenience.
 "I was okay until one day a neighbor kid hollered through the fence, 'How ya doing, blindy'. It was then I began to realize it wasn't that I couldn't see but I was alienated from life. I had to struggle just to be equal. All I wanted was for the kids on the block to say I could play, and co-exist alongside them.
 "I wanted to play Little League Baseball and so much wanted to pitch. I practiced in the backyard with a kid who would hit his glove and I'd pitch to the sound.
 "Let me tell you about my first game. You won't believe me. I struck out the first batter on 3 balls, walked the second and third batters,

and the fourth got a hit and the bases were loaded. The next batter reached the count of 3-2 and my whole life was before my eyes. I wound up, hurled the ball and heard the sound of wood hitting leather. . . . That was the end of my baseball career!

"I got intelligent and turned to wrestling. I lost the first six matches then went on to win 394 in a row."

Learn to take your inconvenience and turn it around and make it a positive force. When we give to help people with an inconvenience, and all people have inconveniences, we allow people to live with us, to co-exist.

Make your inconveniences work for you.

Tom said he wrestled a kid from the Soviet Union and the guy was bashing his head in. He wondered, "What can I do and get out of here without my head being bloodied my and skull being cracked?" So he squeezed out one of his plastic eyes and hollered, "Stop, stop, stop!"

"Why?" the Russian kid asked? "I lost my eye!" The Russian gulped, got up, left the arena and Tom Sullivan won the match by default.

"I also used to drop that eye in ladies drinks and say, 'Here's looking at you, sweetheart.'"

"Laugh at yourself, not your situation. At Harvard in 1966 when all the lights went out, I got a bullhorn and went to the main quad and told them: 'The blacks aren't taking over, nor the Commies, but the most oppressed people of all, the blind people, are taking over.' Other people began to laugh with me."

"I have two children", said Tom. At the time Karen was nine and Bligh was seven. "We moved to California and a neighbor kid said 'Your Dad is blind.' "What is blind?" Bligh said: "Blind means Dad can't see but God taught him other stuff."

"One day, holding on to my daughter's hand, I took her swimming in a neighbor's pool. Suddenly, the phone rang and I got out of the pool, letting go of her hand as I did so. The next thing I knew I heard a splash as she fell into the pool. In a moment of horror all my life flashed before me. I thought: 'Here it is . . . all the struggling of your kid drowning and you can't do anything about it 'cause you're blind.' I said, 'Oh God, will you help me? God, will you help me?'

"Then I heard the sound of air bubbles coming up through water and I found her. Thank God, she's alive today—a beautiful girl."

Sightless Tom Sullivan *saw* and called out his inner strength. Can we?

Tom wrote a song with the line, "Beauty is in the eye of the beholder."

Can we begin to see the beauty all around us today and the beauty within each person?

Can we recognize each person as a unique and gallant spirit? Throw away labels: old, young, black, white? Come to terms with honest realities? Relish a walk in the sun as much as a stock portfolio?

Have we really begun to tap the potential resources within each of us?

Can we master the art of living 'in between'?

PRAYER:

God, grant me:
the serenity to accept the things I cannot change,
the courage to change the things I can,
and the wisdom to distinguish the one from the other.

Amen.

The Road From Defeat To Victory

"I am persuaded . . . that nothing shall separate us from the love of God in Christ Jesus our Lord."

Romans 8:39

No person enjoys being defeated. We want respect from others, as well as self respect. Everybody wants to be somebody. I was reminded of this in a newsstory of a young man caught robbing a bank. The police officer asked, "Why did you want to rob the bank?" He replied, "I just wanted to be somebody." Out of work for weeks, he had no money. He felt defeated. "Just got to thinking if I had some money in my pocket I'd feel like somebody."

I know a lot of people with money in their pocket who acknowledge that money is not the answer to man's deep longings. There are no treasures on earth that make us happy.

Life's a constant struggle. We battle financial hardships, sickness, sorrow, fears, moments of defeat. It is difficult at times to see any light of hope in the future. Every person comes sooner or later to a point in life where he feels defeated. I want to suggest three things to remember when we face what appears to be unconquerable problems.

(1) What shall we then say to these things? [Rom. 8:31] How will we face perplexing problems of life? **Our attitude toward life will defeat us much faster than our burdens.** I know some who have given up in defeat when the common storms of life descended. I know others who have faced what appeared to be more than their share of heartaches, yet have managed to keep a Christian perspective of life.

Paul took the attitude that we're not alone. He said, "I am persuaded neither death nor life shall separate us from the love of God." [38-39] Those whose faith is firmly anchored in the goodness of God never fail to pass successfully through dark ways of life into the light of God's love.

I've seen many people triumph over sorrow because of a Christian attitude. A man sat in my office after learning that his father was dying. We prayed and we asked God to give his family courage and hope for the hours ahead. Instead of blaming God for his loss, the man said, "We are mighty thankful God let us have him so long. We hate to give him up but we know God has been good to us." He was able to count his blessings, even through tears of sorrow.

How different from the man who was released from Oakland County jail and five hours later sought to kill a woman saying, "Someone killed my mother, I want to kill someone else's mother." Though he had tied her hands and dragged her through the house, thank God police came before he carried out the threat.

(2) Paul said, "If God be for us, who can be against us." [Romans 8:31] He was urging us to look at the problems of life against the backdrop of God's power. We need to take our minds off our problems and think about the power that is available to us. What enemy can prevail over us if we march with God? You may be certain that no situation in life is hopeless, because God's power is greater than all the burdens, heartaches, problems and sins that we can know.

(3) Let's remember the answer Paul received to his prayer when he asked God to remove his thorn in the flesh: "My grace is sufficient for thee." [II Cor. 12:9] Little wonder Paul preached the power of God. When Paul said, "I can do all things through Christ who strengthens me." [Phil. 4:13] that was not mere philosophical theory or theological conjecture. Those words didn't fall like pious platitudes from the lips of one who had spent most of his life on the battlefield. Paul knew what it was like to be despised, forsaken, beaten, shipwrecked, cast into prison. He knew the power of Rome and the demands of the Christian life. He had discovered something else. He knew the POWER OF GOD and *that* made the difference.

Face life fortified with the knowledge that God never forgets us. Those who have walked mountain peaks of achievement, enjoyed the thrill of success, have also stumbled through valleys of disappointment and hard work.

Working in his lab at 2 a.m., Thomas Edison had a smile on his face. Seeing the smile, his assistant shouted, "You've solved it. You have the answer." Edison replied, "Not a blamed thing works; but now I can start over again." He knew hundreds of defeats before he discovered the thrill of success. Edward Gibbon took twenty years to write the *Decline and Fall of the Roman Empire*.

In a Christian philosophy one must make room for the inevitable experiences of life. Though not a pleasant thought, all will die; no one gets out of here alive. Most of us will know the loneliness and deep sorrow which comes when we lose someone close to us. In those times the Christian knows God hasn't deserted us; He is near—to comfort and guide us. Christian faith teaches us that death, as well as life, is God's plan.

A Christian is not exempt from the burdens of life and its hardships. Dr. Joseph Parker was an eminent British minister of another generation. He was debating at Hyde Park, Speakers Corner, when an unbeliever shouted, "What did Christ do for Stephen when he was stoned?" Dr. Parker replied, "He gave him grace to pray for those who stoned him." Stephen was martyred but he was not defeated. He stands today as a symbol of what the power of God can do for those who fight the battles of life in the heat of the day.

When Jesus saw Simon Peter and Andrew casting their net into the sea, He invited them to become His disciples. He said, "Follow me, and I will make you fishers of men." [Matt. 4:18-19] He constantly invited people to follow him. "Deny yourself, take up your cross and follow me." [Mark 8:34] He never promised to keep us free from temptations of life. He didn't say: "Follow me and I will make you . . . " So, what did He mean?

I believe He meant that He would make us equal to the demands of the day. Surely he meant He'd make us strong enough to bear the burdens of life.

Lazarus died, Mary & Martha were filled with great sorrow and friends gathered to comfort them. The presence of friends supports us during such a time, but only God can bring comfort to our hearts.

Mary met Jesus outside of town and talked with Him. She knew that her sister's heart was breaking with grief, so she went quickly to the house and said to Mary, "The Master is here and is calling for you." [John 11:28]

I believe God calls every person. He speaks to us in His persuasive way in an effort to get us to follow Him. He does not call all of us to be pastors or missionaries but He calls us all; He calls us to be genuinely Christian. He calls some of us to do certain things, but He calls each of us to *be* a certain kind of person. What you *are* is far more important than what you *do*.

That is to say, you may be a street-sweeper or a heart surgeon, but the difference that determines your destiny is not what you do, but what you are. I would rather pick up the debris left by a thoughtless humanity while walking in the footsteps of God than sleep in the bed of a king, eat from sterling silver plates, and drink from golden goblets while holding the hand of Satan.

Everyone has failed at some time or other. No serious minded person claims his or her life has been perfect. Our spiritual failure is reflected in war, crime, divorce, hypocrisy. The road from spiritual failure to triumphant living is not an easy road to travel. As Pete Rose, the Cincinnati Reds all-star said following his conviction on gambling charges, "I am going to pay the fine, serve the sentence, do the community service, put my life back together and get on with life." I thought, "Good for you, Pete, but you'll not put it together the way it

could be, if you try to put it back together without God."
     The Christian life is not stumbled upon by accident. It is achieved only with divine grace and diligent human effort. I suggest four steps to move from spiritual failure to triumphant living.
     (1) Take a look within. How long has it been since you gave some serious thought to your life. A month, a year, never. We're constantly changing. In taking a trip recently I found it necessary to check the road map frequently or I'd have been lost. Life is like that. Each day we travel a road that is unfamiliar to us. We meet new opportunities and challenges. We face new battles and different problems. We need a spiritual road map to guide us safely through the perplexing problems of each day. Jesus said, "I am the way, the truth and the life." [John 14:6] In Christ we have our best Example and Guide.
     I have a friend who says, "I'm not a religious man." He doesn't really have to say that, it shows. He has some health problems, goes once a week to his doctor, has a complete checkup every three months. I don't quarrel with that. Talking one day about life and urging him to get closer to God, I said, "Bill, if you were half as concerned with your soul as you are with your gall bladder, you'd be a much better fellow." I don't think he liked hearing me say that but I think it got him thinking.
     Every person ought to examine his or her life in light of two important questions:
     First: What am I doing that I know is out of harmony with the life and teachings of Jesus? This is very much like going to a doctor. A good doctor will make every effort to localize the difficulty and try to discover the cause.
     Next: Examine your life in light of another question: What can I do to improve my life?
     Actually, this is the second thing a physician will do once he has made a diagnosis of an illness. The doctor wants to make the patient well again. A businessman would be foolish if he didn't spend some time each week trying to determine better ways of doing the job. Competition demands it.
     Let me be quick to add that self-examination is not sufficient to move one from spiritual failure to triumphant living. It is only the first step. It is not enough to know what is wrong with one's life and to discover ways to improve it. Other steps are essential.
     (2) You must want to be a better person; then you must work toward that end. Can I tell you a secret desire of mine. I have always wanted to play the piano. We didn't have a piano in our home but a 75 year-old neighbor did. I would spend evenings at her house so I could

play the piano. Unfortunately, she went to bed with the chickens and got up with them. I never progressed farther than "Chopsticks", "Sweet Hour of Prayer", "Bringing in the Sheaves" and a few measures of "Dark Eyes". I had a desire to play the piano but I also worked on the farm from sun-up to sun-down. Whenever I got a few spare minutes, I found I was more interested in playing with the other kids on the adjacent farm than I was in going to Miss Delia's to play the piano. The result? I never learned to play the piano.

You do not learn to live triumphantly by merely desiring it any more than you learn to play the piano by desiring it. To become an accomplished pianist you must spend many hours with some fine music teacher and many more hours at the keyboard practicing. If you would climb to the heights of triumphant living you will spend some time with the Master. You are willing to let Him make you a 'fisher of souls'.

In 1992 we celebrated the 500th anniversary of Columbus' finding a new continent. Columbus had spent many years trying to get someone to believe in him and back him financially. If he had not been a man of perseverance he'd have deserted his dream. For 18 long years, Columbus worked untiringly amid poverty, neglect, and ridicule, trying to solicit funds for his mission. The prime of his life was spent in the struggle but as a result he was able to set sail from Palos on August 3, 1492. His desire plus his determined effort finally brought him success.

Columbus fought against heavy odds when his crew didn't cooperate with him. They pleaded with him to turn back and then threatened mutiny. They had lost faith in the venture. That didn't shake Columbus determination: he made the same entry in his diary day after day, "This day we sailed on." He did not say, "We have reached our destination."

You and I haven't reached many of our goals. We are not yet the person we had hoped to become. Let us continue to write in our spiritual diaries: "This day I sailed on. I will continue to sail on toward worthy ports as God gives me another tomorrow." The fellow who pulls in his oars and takes down his sail cannot expect to reach the safety of the harbor. The person who loses his desire and determination will never win a worthwhile battle in life.

(3) We must repent of our wrongs and accept God's forgiveness. Repent is a word that has dropped out of our vocabulary. I say *repent* rather than *confess*. To confess is to acknowledge. We need to do more than simply confess. We need God's forgiveness. I know people who live constantly aware of their sins but make little effort to attain God's forgiveness.

The word, repent, is a strong word which clearly implies

confession. Repentance is two-fold: it means to turn away from and forsake sin; it means one reaches out toward God. Forgiveness involves both God and the person. It is through God's mercy and love that forgiveness is possible. Man can't redeem himself. It's God's work. Your parents, your pastor can't do it for you. It is a personal experience.

Harry Denman, the great Methodist lay evangelist, preached in a revival meeting. He was invited to stay in a lovely home and when the thoughtful hostess showed him to the room he'd occupy for the week, she remarked: "Brother Denman, this is the room in which my grandmother prayed." Harry Denman replied in his tender fashion, "I'm glad to know where your grandmother prayed. But, where do you pray?"

The crucial issue is not so much where our parents or grandparents stood in relation to God, but where do we stand. Our destiny is determined not by their goodness but by our own. I never tire hearing people talk about the consecration and loyalty of their relatives, **but we must face the fact that we can't get to heaven on their recommendation.**

(4) To live triumphantly we must anchor our trust in God. I see many people who seem to be indifferent to God, living as if they do not need Him. While enjoying the warm sunshine of good health and the gentle breeze of prosperity, I remind you that in every life some shadows will fall. Night will come and unless we have a light of faith we will stumble and fall.

Vern Good was an elderly, devoted member of this congregation. He told the story of being on a passenger vessel steaming ahead at full speed on the St. Lawrence River. On deck, he and some other passengers became frightened when the vessel ran into some thick fog. One complained to the first mate that the captain was careless. The sailor smiled and said, "Don't be afraid. The fog lies low, but the captain is high above it and can see where we are going."

There are times in life when we can't see where we are going. But God is piloting us. Let's not be afraid. He stands high on the bridge, above the fog of this earth, and He can see where we are going. Trust Him.

Life takes us across valleys, mountains, bridges, and chasms. Part of the journey is smooth and easy; part is rugged and difficult.

If you carry only logic with you, it will take you part of the way; but somewhere on the road of life logic will leave you stranded.

If you take only knowledge, far from heaven's gates you will become weary and exhausted.

You may choose to take reason, but reason's light will grow dim before the journey is over.

These are all good companions. I would expect a good Christian to take them all. But they are not sufficient.

The sun may shine tomorrow in your life, or the clouds may descend, but with faith in God you can be triumphant. **Amen.**

Everything is possible to one who has faith. Jesus said, "If you are able!—all things can be done for the one who believes." [Mark 9:23]

The Power Is In The 'Yes'!

"Finally, brethren, whatever is true, honorable, just, pure, gracious, if there is any excellence, if there is anything worthy of praise, think on these things."

Philippians 4:8

There are a lot of people who think that Lent is a negative season. Lent is a time to let go of something in your life you're doing that you ought not to be doing or to give up something that ought to be given up—to remind you of the One who gave up his life for us all, Jesus Christ. But I want to begin Lent by reminding you that Lent is not a season in which to say, "No". It is a season in which we are called to say, "Yes". And the ***power*** . . . is in the "***YES!***"

Most of us grew up with negative religion, a series of don'ts: "Don't do this; don't do that". A man from England had moved to Detroit. Knowing how strong Methodism had been in England I asked him in what church did he 'grow up.' It's a question I ask a lot of people. He said, "I 'grew up' Methodist" then quickly added, "but I grew up so restricted in what I could or couldn't do that I determined when I got out from under my father's roof, I would do as I pleased, and that *would **not** include* going to Church. "And Reverend," he said rather boastfully, "it hasn't!" as if to say, "You need not invite me to your church. I won't be there."

Negative religion.

When I was in high school and college, I joined the debate team. In thinking about this, recalling the issues we debated—the abolition of the electoral college and a direct vote of the people in presidential elections among them, it occurred to me that in high school and college, I was never assigned the *negative* position. I always thought the *affirmative* side of the debate was the more difficult. It was the side that I was on, the argument that I was arguing. Every seasoned debater knows it is always easier to tear down another person's argument than to present a positive case of your own. It is easier to tear people down than it is to build them up. It is easier to criticize people and what they're doing than to constructively attempt to do it yourself. *Negatives* are more numerous than positives in our language. We are much more vocal in setting forth what we are against than in setting forth what we are *for*. "I'll tell you what I'm against!". . . and we begin to reel it off. And yet, here is Paul saying, "My brothers and sisters, whatever is true, whatever is honorable, whatever is just, whatever is pure, whatever is gracious"—all positives—"if there be any excellence, if there be anything worthy of praise, think on these things." [Phil. 4:8]

It's time our society begins to take this matter seriously. I think of the theater for the past 30 or 40 years. The *Theater* has become a platform for negativism. Some twenty years ago Robert Lee wrote :

> The marvel to me is that so many millions of people will actually pay money for the fermenting garbage in a playwright's mind. A portion of our theater today has fallen to a tribe of quasi-Freudians who think garbage is a great discovery. And there seem to be some ticket buyers who have lived such pure, sheltered, sterilized lives that they are willing to pay to see what dirt looks like.

Or, look at much of literature. An article in the *Saturday Review* focused on a critic who reviewed the case against the literary avant-garde with their emphasis on violence, perversion and nihilism that seems rooted in contempt for the world. The critic, a man by the name of Joseph Kruth, came to this conclusion about much of modern literature:

> Seldom, if ever before, has any of the arts been so dominated by an all exclusive hatred. Once, the writer hated the individual 'bad man'. Then he began to hate instead the 'society' which was supposed to be responsible for the creation of the bad men. Now this hatred is directed not at individuals or their societies but at the 'universe' in which bad men and bad societies are merely fundamental expressions of the fundamental evil of the universe itself.

The most common response to the question, 'What is fundamental?' he concludes, is 'the taste for violence.' The belief that violence is the only appropriate response to an absurd world is the one element often present in literature today. We know it. All we have to do is watch the movies, sit down at night and watch the television, read the daily newspaper, and witness the violence unleashed in the city and in our society.

The forces of negativism are loose in our society and attempting to crush the human spirit. We are assaulted on all sides, by a series of negations. This is why it is crucial for the Church to *be there* with the GOOD NEWS and for each Christian to take this problem seriously, in a personal way in his or her own life.

Let's talk about the negative person. Negative persons, I have found, are always unhappy and unpleasant persons. They are the antagonists in the Church. There is nothing winsome or attractive at all in the kind of person who, when he has the choice between two evils, chooses both. George Bernard Shaw commented with caustic wit that a negative person is one who thinks everybody else is as "nasty as himself and hates them for it."

The negative person says "No" to life because he looks at life with an insistent "No". He criticizes the community, is down on the Church, claims the schools are inadequate, usually puts doctors, lawyers and teachers in the same bag and is irritated at all three. He believes society is doomed, government is corrupt, wars are inevitable, racial conflicts inescapable and things in general all over the world are in an impossible mess. Is it any wonder that negative people walk alone, go to lunch alone, sit at home night after night alone? The negative person, the person who says "No" to life, is going to be an unhappy and unpleasant person.

The *power* is in the *"yes."*

The *negative* person's attitude is contrary to the spirit of Jesus—a magnificently positive person. His message was marvelously life affirming. All of His teachings gathered up together will stand up and shout: **"LIFE IS GOOD!"** He made it perfectly clear that His purpose in coming to earth was to offer the more abundant life to all who would accept it.

This is what He believed: life is not something to be endured but something to be enjoyed. Life is not to be endured in dread, but to be lived in delight. Life is not ugly, though there is ugliness to it and in it, to be sure. Rather, life is essentially beautiful.

Humankind is not wholly wicked. There are evil men and women but mankind is essentially noble. There is hatred, but there is also love. There is greed, but there is also unselfishness . . . and there is more out there if we would only open our eyes to see it. There is filth, but there is also purity.

Jesus calls us to run out and embrace life. He summons us from our morbid moments of negativism to dash out of ourselves and greet life. Thus, the negative person by his or her very nature is living far afield from Jesus Christ. A Christian ought to be an essentially happy person.

And while I do not know of any claim he made to be a Christian, (although certainly a symbol of hedonism), I was fascinated by the news that Malcolm Forbes chose his own epitaph: ***"While alive, he lived!"*** Can that be said of us as Christians?

This is not to say that a Christian may expect to be unacquainted with grief and a stranger to sorrow. Nor is it to suggest that joy is never tempered by sadness. But it is to say that there is a fundamental contradiction in the person who professes to be a Christian and at the same time goes around an unhappy person.

From the South comes an old story of a grandfather whose

grandson observed, "Grandpa, you know, our mule is a good Christian." And his grandfather said, "What do you mean?" "Well you know, Grandpa, he has such a long face!"

That's not what Christianity is all about.

Our world is contaminated with negations. An individual who becomes a negative person is unhappy with himself and is an unattractive person to others. Further, an unhappy person who calls himself or herself a Christian could be a walking contradiction.

So let's set down briefly some affirmations—affirmations which will enable you to finally say *"Yes!"*—not only in Lent but in all of life.

First, let our positive attitudes be so deliberately developed and so habit-disciplined they become absorbed into our lives as a part of our very being.

I had a wonderful time sharing with sixty pastors of larger churches in the Western North Carolina Conference. I was a house guest of the Bishop, a man whose optimism every Methodist Bishop would do well to imitate, at least in spirit. He enjoys life, enjoys the ministry, enjoys people. He came in one evening with two loaves of freshly baked bread. The next morning we sat down at the table. He, himself, prepared our breakfast. As we were sitting there, he sliced the bread, and went quickly from the table to get the Conference Journal. He came back, found the telephone number of the preacher who baked the bread and rang him up. "Erman," he said, "this is Bev Jones and I want you to know you are feeding your Bishop this morning and also a pastor with whom you worked in 1956." (A student on a Duke Endowment Summer Internship in 1956.)

I have roomed with him at various Methodist Conferences around the world and knew him before he was elected a Bishop. His thoughtfulness and thankful heart—so typical of his positive outlook on life and about people—spoke volumes!

An old New England story is told about a man with a poor reputation who died. They asked the Methodist preacher to conduct his funeral. He declined saying, "I won't do it. He was a ne'er do well." They asked the Baptist Preacher to have the funeral and he said, "No, I can't do it, he wasn't a Christian." They asked the Unitarian preacher if he would have it. He said, "Yes, I will . . . gladly." Practically everyone in the town turned out for the funeral, many out of curiosity wondering what the Unitarian pastor would say about this ne'er do well. He stood in the pulpit and in his eulogy he said, "There's only one thing I can say about our friend. *He was not as mean **all** the time as he was **some** of the time!"*

Find something good to say. Build the positive into your

personality. Let it be absorbed into your very being. For, "As one thinketh in one's heart, so one is." That's not only biblical truth, its good psychological truth.

I received a call from a friend down South, the president of a wholesale house. The year before he had faced the possibility of bankruptcy. But now, he stands on firm financial ground. He is devoting his energies and wealth to many good and worthy causes. In fact, the whole conversation was not about how he saved his business but what he is doing in that Carolina community. I asked him how he was able to turn his life and his business around at a very critical time, and he said: "Bill, I believe with all my heart any person can do almost anything that he really believes in and wants to do. I *believe* the Bible when it says, 'I can do all things through Christ who strengthens me.'"

The Bible does not mean that we can do everything in the world. I can't fly an airplane. I can't play eighteen holes of golf. But the Bible *is* saying that whatever it is I *need* to do, *I can do—through Christ who strengthens me.*

What a powerful truth! It will help you out of unhappiness and defeat, of this I am sure. I have seen it operative in the one who has been a chronic failure and in the one who has been an unfailing achiever. Let your attitudes, deliberately developed and habit-disciplined, stand strong over an affirmation of life when you follow in the footsteps of Jesus.

For a second step, move beyond a wistful nostalgia for the past and hold with a measure of joy, the affirmation of today—yes, this very present day. I don't know who wrote this little doggerel but I remember it from forty-five years ago when I began my ministry and I've seen it proven true time and time again..

> "Our fathers have been churchmen 2000 years or so,
> and to every new suggestion they always answer, 'No'."

That is what is wrong with the Church today in far too many places. We think the past was so wonderful! "Oh, if we could **only** go back to the glory days of this or that preacher when our church was filled, and people were standing in line. You had to come here at 10 o'clock on Sunday morning to get a seat! If only we could get back to those glory days!"

Friends, those days are gone forever. These are not those days and I keep reminding myself, it is more important, by Gods grace, to try to fill the *people* who come to this place . . . than to try to fill the *place*! And if the *people* are filled, maybe one day the *place* will be filled again.

Memory is *selective*, especially where sentiment is involved. We cannot trust ourselves about the past. I heard about a man who reached his 100th birthday and the newspaper sent a young reporter out to interview him. He was asked the inevitable question: 'To what do you attribute your long life?' "Well, son, I attribute it to the fact that it was my good fortune to have been born a century ago." That's just about how reliable some of us are in looking wistfully and nostalgically at the past.

Affirm *today* - not yesterday, not tomorrow, but *today*. Enjoy the present. Do your duty and leave the rest to God. This is all you have to do.

Finally, affirm God. Affirm God in your life now and everyday of the rest of your life.

J.A. Hadfield, a student of psychotherapy, an Englishman, wrote without concern for theology:

> I am convinced the Christian religion is one of the most valuable and potent influences that we possess for producing our harmony, peace of mind and the confidence of soul needed to bring health and power to patients. The Christian religion, the religion of God as He is made known to us through Jesus Christ, is a mighty affirmation of religion as an act of faith.

That confidence, in Dr. Hadfield's words, that confidence of soul, is needed to bring health and power and wholeness.

I do not ask you to give up anything during Lent. But, I do ask you to give in to God, and set yourselves on a path that rises above the negativism of our society into an ultimate *affirmation of Life*.

There is little power in the *'No.'*

The *power*——is in the *'Yes!'*

Rejection:
Life's Hardest Blow

*"I will praise thee for I am
fearfully and wonderfully made."*

Psalm 139:14

I will praise thee for I am fearfully and wonderfully made! Just which of man's impressive credentials prompted this word we do not know. Perhaps it was human durability, our capacity for stress, our ability to take it and keep coming back for more.

The body can absorb a lot of punishment: unrelieved thirst, unwise diet, sleepless nights. The mind is no less durable. It can work without letup for days. It can stretch to receive, store and recall more and more information. It can adjust to new truth. It can grapple gamely with paradox and contradiction.

And the heart of man? Here is the capacity to absorb shock, to hover on the brink of despair and recover, to weather loss, to bear up under the collapse of longheld dreams.

"Fearfully and wonderfully made . . ."

And yet, there is one blow to which humankind is vulnerable. On the strength of both personal and pastoral experience, one feels justified in calling this the hardest blow of all. This is the blow that can erase a man's smile, buckle his knees, stoop his shoulders, snap his mind and even break his heart. The hardest blow of all is to be rejected.

Rejection comes in a variety of forms and faces. It can be real or imagined. One can be rejected by other people. One can imagine himself rejected by God. One can even reject one's own self.

There is such a thing as vocational rejection, as when a person is laid off from work and curtly told that his skill has become an anachronism in today's world.

It is possible for one generation to reject another. As when a son or daughter puts an aging parent on the shelf; or when parents write off a teen-ager because they scorn their life-style and culture. It is possible when a corporation fires a man at age sixty and replaces him with a man of forty. It is possible when a know-it-all young person proclaims mistrust of anyone over thirty.

There can be rejection on the grounds of race. Apparently some people never feel tall enough unless they can put other people under them.

There can be social rejection, a subtle form of caste where people are judged and separated according to their parentage, their ability to amass money or display wealth. *"Can any good thing come out of Nazareth?"* they asked in response to the claims of Jesus. And that was that! . . . *social* rejection!

There can be a rejection of self when a person gives up on himself, grows to hate his own being and becomes a candidate for suicide.

Just how severe a blow rejection is can be measured in at least two ways.

Look first at the lengths to which we go to prevent rejection. Here, I believe, is the root cause of virtually all of our conformity, the fear of being dropped by some group whose esteem and friendship we prize. Rather than risk rejection we compromise our moral, cultural and intellectual standards.

Even the counterculture is not exempt from the urge to conform. There, a smaller public is involved but it is nonetheless demanding. Somerset Maugham in The Moon and Sixpence wrote:

> It isn't difficult to be unconventional in the eyes of the world when your unconventionality is but the convention of your set. It affords you an inordinate amount of self-esteem. You have the self-satisfaction of courage without the inconvenience of danger.

Yes, we go to enormous lengths to prevent rejection and feign acceptance.

Look secondly at the strong reactions that rejection touches off. Baseball fans will remember the name quickly of Elston Howard, who spent most of his active baseball life with the New York Yankees. Astute fans of the sport will remember that towards the end of his career he was traded to Boston. That move jarred the celebrated catcher more than a collision at homeplate. A sports writer who is intimate with Elston Howard said, "It was not moving to Boston that upset him. It was just the thought that after so many successful years as a Yankee he was no longer wanted."

One of the Detroit Tigers' most popular young rookie pitchers was Mark Fidrych. After a couple of successful seasons in the Major League, he was demoted to the Minor League farm team in Lakeland, Florida. Mark, upon hearing the news of his demotion said, "If I can pitch three innings in Lakeland, why not three innings in Detroit?"

Rejection usually touches off a chain reaction that starts with self-pity, moves to sour grapes (*"Who wanted to belong anyway?"*), goes on to bitterness and finally hardens into thoughts of vengeance.

It's my guess that most of the disturbances we've had in our

Rejection: Life's Hardest Blow

prisons and much of our crime are traceable at the bottom to the sin of rejection. Always, of course, there are the surface causes, but underneath is the grim fact of rejection.

It's a soul-shattering experience to come upon the words *'Keep-out'* and know they're meant for you. Keep out of . . . this school, this neighborhood, this beach, this job.

After the civil rights lunch-counter sit-ins of 1962 in Greensboro, North Carolina, I sat down with some of my laymen to talk about blacks being seated when they came to worship. One man led off at a surprisingly naive level. He said, "You know, preacher, we discriminate in every aspect of life. When this church got you as a preacher, the Bishop could have chosen someone else. When you bought that necktie you chose it out of an assortment of ties and rejected others."

I listened and when it came my turn to speak, I had to be firm. I pointed out there is no similarity at all between the rejection of particular neckties and the rejection of particular people. The essential nature of a necktie is not affected by rejection. A human being has his psyche badly wounded by rejection. His value as a person is assaulted.

What does the Christian faith have to say about rejection?

For one thing it affirms our need to live in relationship with others. It is not good for man to be alone. Has it ever struck you as significant that there is no formal, abstract definition of God in the Bible? Rather, God is always presented in Scripture in His various relationships: to nature, to nations, to men and women. . . *"Adam, where art thou?"* [Genesis 3:9]

Even more striking is the fact that there is no formal definition of man in the Bible. Man as well as God is disclosed in Scripture, even defined, if you will, in terms of his relationships: hiding, fashioning fig leaves, making idols, worshipping, always in relationship. This is how we know who we are and what we are. Our estrangement from each other is the clearest indication of our fallenness.

Moreover, in the face of our fear of rejection, the Christian faith proclaims the steadfast love of God. One of America's favorite cowboys ended his performances by saying somewhat breezily, "May the good Lord take a likin' to ya", as though there was some doubt about the constancy of God's affection.

God's relationship to us is not capricious or whimsical. He has covenanted his love toward us. He has pledged to love us with an everlasting love.

The Prodigal Son returns home expecting to be rejected by his father. Instead, he is lovingly accepted. When we suffer the unspeakable pain of rejection—let the words come back—let the truth come home—*God loves us!* He accepts us as we are. Our striving must be only to accept His acceptance of us.

What else does the Christian faith have to say about rejection? It presents us with a Savior who Himself experienced rejection. "He was despised and rejected of men," says Isaiah 53:3. It is conceivable that this verse initially had reference to a king and perhaps to the nation itself, but it is inconceivable that this chapter is lacking all references to Jesus. "He was despised and rejected of men."

He was unwanted—by church, government, society. He came to His own and his own received him not. He had no place to lay his head. He died on a cross, suspended between Heaven and earth, as if wanted by neither. From the cross, he cried, "My God, My God, why have you forsaken me?" [Matt. 27:46] not so much to bemoan his pain as to express his sense of rejection and separation.

This is more than one of the 'inconveniences of greatness', as someone has put it, as though Jesus were rejected only in the sense that he lived ahead of his time. I don't know what your Christian theology is, but any Christian theology that would reduce the feeling of rejection that Jesus knew to a theological fiction is untrue. His rejection was real, every bit as real as ours.

What stands to arrest our attention is the fact that when He was rejected, Jesus didn't react like we react.

He didn't indulge in self-pity, engage in sour grapes, become embittered, or stoop to vengeance. The writer of the Epistle to the Hebrews knew the why of it all: "Because he himself has suffered and been tempted, he is able to help those who are tempted." [Hebrews 2:17-18]

Finally, faith has this to say: God in his mercy sets the rejected ones of earth into a community in which each receives the other as all have been received by God. The climate of any authentic congregation is controlled by the love of God. Acceptance is not conditioned upon whether someone qualifies, by the size of the purse, the impressiveness of his achievements, or by his moral rectitude.

The invitation is always there to come as you are. This does not mean that Jesus, in receiving us, approves of us as we are. Acceptance and approval are not the same. In fact, disapproval can be a form of acceptance, can it not?

Frequently, one hears it said that the Church is simply a pragmatic way for people who believe alike to get things done. In the little book, *God With Us*, the author comes closer to the truth when he writes, "They are together not only for accomplishing common purposes, but also for being present one to another, to be really there when the other needs us."

Rejection: Life's Hardest Blow

A nine year old girl said one time in an essay for her teacher: "I don't know exactly what a family is, but I know one thing. Your friends can go off and say they don't want to be your friends anymore, but family just can't go off and say they don't want to be your family anymore." That is what God intends his church to be—a family in which each receives the other as all have been received by God.

The hardest blow is rejection.

I read about a chief engineer on a freighter who had filled the zoo in his hometown in Germany with specimens of God's creation from around the world. He personally brought in crocodiles, alligators, poisonous snakes. He was asked, "How do you do it?"

He replied, "It's simple. If I have a boa constrictor I'm bringing home from India, I feed it two or three rabbits. The reptile devours them instantly, then curls up and sleeps until I get it home." I thought, 'How remarkable!' The animal has had enough to eat. Its anxieties cease and it's at peace.

But that isn't true of a human being. Man is different. After we've had enough to eat, and our primary physical satisfactions are attended to, our worries only begin. This is because we are made for each other. One of our cardinal worries has to do with rejection. In fact, this fear is so strong in us that we often choose not to take a stand, to be a wall flower, to stay on the edges, otherwise we might get hurt.

There may be someone reading these words who is caught in depression—the inevitable result of rejection. Anger and bitterness may seem the only way to respond. I have three words for you: **God loves you.**

Jesus understands you.

The Church is ready to receive you—just as you are!

PRAYER:

Lord, we pray for all who are caught in the hopeless cycle of rejection, resentment and retaliation. Let your saving and delivering word have its way among us. Help those who know You to be better models of your love. Fashion us into a healing and restoring fellowship, through the same Jesus Christ, our Lord, who loved us and gave Himself for us. Amen.

Running Life's Race To Win!

*"This one thing I do;
forgetting all that lies behind,
I press on towards the goal
of the prize of the upward call of God
in Christ Jesus."*
I Corinthians 9:24-27

I believe that we are created for achievement. Something in us wants to run faster, jump higher, swim further, build bigger and create more. There's a sense of creativity and achievement seething within the hearts of men and women.

Recently I sought to review the old Olympic records. There seemed to be not one field or track event where people run, jump, throw, vault, leap or hurdle, where the world record is older than four years. In other words, every world record is broken again and again. Athletes seek and strive for yet another record.

Although this is true in athletics, it's also true in other fields of life. People want to sell more, make more money, build bigger barns and better homes. Many know the pressure at work to sell more, to buy more. to push harder, to achieve more, to create more. Each one of us is constantly under some type of pressure. The interesting thing about it is that unless we have more of a sense of achievement, we don't have a deep sense of satisfaction.

How sad it is that while there are many successful, affluent, able, competent, self-confident people who are successful achievers, there are many people who never achieve anything. They seem to be 'born losers'. There are people who never seem to come in first; they always come in second, third or fourth. They are on the sideline, or find themselves always on the bench. These people are not winners. They struggle with a sense that they are born to lose. They have a strong sense of their inferiority. They are society's classic 'losers'.

No person ever develops a sense of self-sufficiency and self-worth until achieving something. I believe there is built into our human nature something that cries out for recognition and achievement. Each of us needs at some point, sometime, somewhere, to experience victory.

The Apostle Paul spoke of striving in order to succeed at being effective people. In I Corinthians 9:24-27, Paul uses the word which means, "As one competing in the game." He was writing to Corinth, the home of the Isthmian Games, the second most important games in all of Greece, second only to the Olympic Games. Every three years, athletes from all over Greece would come together at Corinth in the great Stadia to compete for prizes together. The Apostle Paul reminded the church at Corinth that they had a responsibility as Christians to learn to grow and to be effective in their spiritual life, and learn spiritually how to win.

Paul wrote: "Run then in such a way that you will win." If you want to be a person who is on the winning side, to be an effective outgoing person, then you run your race to win. Strive to have success.

Fear of failure robs people of success. Our two youngest sons have been track enthusiasts and each qualified for their high school track and cross-country teams. At their events I've seen runners at the sound of the starting gun get off a substantial lead and then, when caught by other runners and passed by, begin to fade. I remember one runner who, once he was overtaken by another runner, began a slightly longer lope with his left leg and there ensued an unrhythmical stride. He slowed, the others ran ahead. Shortly, he pulled out of the race rubbing his thigh.

I was commenting to a bystander who replied, "Oh that's known as the loser's limp. It means as soon as you see you are being overtaken and you are not going to win, you begin to build your excuse for your failure at that moment; you start limping before you get to the finish line."

People who fail, frequently spend more effort on developing a system of loser's limps than they do of ever succeeding. I want to tell you there is nothing to fear about failure. There is more fear about not attempting than there is about failure.

If you want to be successful, you have to dream about it. Dreams cost you nothing. If you build a dream, you will find your dream will build you. If you have a desire to achieve, you are willing to risk.

Whether you want to write a book or a poem, to assemble a car engine or be a successful salesman, you start to risk and build within yourself the energy that will lead to accomplishment. Having dreamed and dared, you make a start.

Most people never become successful in what they attempt because they never start. They spend their time thinking about beginning rather than commencing to do something.

Recently I discovered a lovely Chinese poem:

Spring is past, Summer has gone; and the Winter is here;
And the song that I was meant to sing is still unsung.
I have spent my days stringing and unstringing my instrument.

There are people everywhere who never get around to doing

anything except spending their time stringing and unstringing their instrument. They never play a melody in their life. They are losers because they never make a departure toward building their dream.

Once you depart you strive for the finish. Paul uses that word time-after-time in that passage. Five times in his letters, the Apostle Paul speaks about life as a race. He speaks of life as a fight or a wrestle. For these things energy is needed.

Unless you dream, dare, depart and push forward, how can you expect to achieve? Only those who learn to aim for something in life will have a sense of purpose. You then persist on going forward, determined to win. It's always too soon to quit. Those who achieve are those who have kept on 'keeping on'.

The Apostle Paul, speaking of himself as an athlete, says "And so I run the race set before me and I run to win, and like any athlete in training I keep my body under strict discipline." (v. 25) If you want to succeed in what you are doing, you always keep your body under strict discipline.

There is self-control in the way you live. Effective people are people who have about them a discipline: a discipline of their speech, their behavior, and of the way they relate to other people. People who are losers have been intemperate in their lifestyle: in their behavior and in their lack of self-discipline.

There needs to be discipline in the way we behave. If we want to be an effective Christian we must develop a sense of discipline just like an athlete.

It takes discipline to be a Christian. You make the Bible a part of your life. Make a list of those things for which you should pray and the people for whom you should pray and pray earnestly. You worship God even on the Sundays when the weather is not to your liking. You worship together with God's people sharing around the communion table of our Lord. You learn to give of your money and talent, developing a generous spirit, and become part of the ongoing work of the mission of Jesus Christ. You learn to witness to other people.

If you lose that sense of self-discipline, you lose the sense of achievement in your spiritual life. Paul goes on to say: "I fix my eye on the line, and I run through to the finish." (v.26) He had a goal. He had an aim, a target. I always suggest to people if you know what your target is, you are more likely to hit it.

Many people never win at anything, always losers, ineffective, never achieving in any area of their life because they have no goal, no target, no purpose, no direction. They are like that man about whom Stephen Leacock wrote: "He flung himself upon his horse and rode off madly in all directions."

Any worthwhile achievement in life comes as a result of reaching set goals. Paul spoke about his goal: "This one thing I do," he said, "forgetting all that lies behind, I press on toward the goal of the prize of the upward call of God in Christ Jesus."

He had one goal, one vision, one objective . . . to grow more like Jesus. He continued that verse: "And I urge those of you who are mature to be thus minded." [Philippians 3:12-15] Those of us who are mature must have a spiritual goal, in order to strive for the upward call of God in Christ Jesus.

Paul concluded, "I bring my body under complete control lest I find myself being disqualified, having already brought other people into the faith, I myself might be a castaway or a disqualified person." He had to complete the course.

We know some people in this life who never grow spiritually; despair with a sense of defeat because they never attain a goal whether it be Bible study, prayer, sharing or witnessing.

May I suggest that if you want to be effective begin achieving some things now by finishing something that you have planned and undertaken. You will not obtain a sense of significance and self-worth until you finish something you have set out to do.

Set yourself an achievable goal and by the grace and power of God believe: "I can do all things through Christ who strengthens me." No matter how difficult the course, don't quit, but finish it. When you finish a course you will find a new sense of self-sufficiency, self-worth and a new sense of dignity.

Paul, having reached the end of his life, could look back and say with a sense of satisfaction, "I have run the race, fought the fight, kept the faith, henceforth there is laid up for me a crown of righteousness." [II Timothy 4:7] Why? Because he had kept going right to the end. Jesus says: "He who endures to the end shall be saved." [Mark 13:13b]

There's a very real sense if you want to be effective and accomplish something in your Christian life, you have to achieve and follow through to the end. It is always too soon to quit.

As part of the family of God, each of us can have an equal role as a child of God. We do that by keeping our eye upon Jesus, by sharing His life, His faith and His victory.

He achieved and so can we when we share with Him. The truth is none of us are 'born losers'. No one else can do anything with the ability God has given you except yourself. How you use that ability will either lead to loss or to victory.

"Therefore, since we are surrounded by so great a cloud of witnesses, let us also lay aside every weight and the sin that clings so

closely, and let us run with perseverance the race that is set before us, looking to Jesus the pioneer and perfector of our faith, who for the sake of the joy that was set before him endured the cross, disregarding its shame, and has taken his seat at the right hand of the throne of God." [Hebrews 12:1-2]

When your eyes are fixed upon Jesus, when you look full in His wonderful face, then in your own heart and life you have His grace and His strength, and through His cross you become the victor. AMEN.

The Goodness of God

*"O give thanks to the LORD, for he is good;
for his steadfast love endures forever."*
Psalm 106:1

*"But God proves his own love for us in that
while we were still sinners, Christ died for us."*
Romans 5:8

I am not unaware that some people in our congregation are in deep water today. Some walk even now through the valley of the shadow of death; others are facing a critical juncture in their lives; still others know themselves to be adrift on some open sea without a rudder or even an anchor to keep them from crashing against the rocks. There are even those who feel God has *deserted* them or perhaps taken a *leave of absence*. God is, somehow, *missing in action*.

I want to say only one thing to you today. The message is singular, but I will say it in three or four ways. It is especially for people in deep water. The message, simply put, is this: **God is *for* us!**

Even when everything else seems to have teamed up against us on the other side of the line of scrimmage, **God is *for* us!** And *"If God be for us, who can be against us?"* [Romans 8:31] If God be *for* us, whoever walks even now through the valley of the shadow of death, need fear no evil. If God be *for* us, whoever faces some critical crossroads in life, need have no anxiety—about anything. If God be *for* us, those whose lives are adrift and headed toward the rocks need not fear nor give up hope in the possibility of new directions.

One of these days I may need you to say those words to me. Today, I am privileged to say them to you, inviting you to trust them with all your heart, mind, soul and strength. And if God **is** for **you** then everything else can be faced, handled, endured, accepted, risked and redeemed.

"O give thanks to the Lord, for He is good; His steadfast love endures forever." [Ps. 106:1]

How do we know the goodness of God? What is the evidence?

First, the Goodness of God is evidenced by the fact that God's love for us does not depend on who we are or what we do. God's love for us is no "quid pro quo." God doesn't say: "I will love you—*if* . . . " God is *for us*, no matter what.

Book titles have always intrigued. Consider this one: *"You Don't Have To Be in 'Who's Who' To Know 'What's What.'"* Rank, title, social class, financial position, race, looks—none of these matters to God. Whoever you are, whatever you own, wherever you live—God loves you! No exceptions!

God's love for you does not depend on your love for Him! God wants you to love Him, but He loves you regardless. God's love doesn't depend on the quality of our faith. God wants us to believe in Him, but He loves the unbeliever just as much as the believer. God's love doesn't depend on personal morality, nor is His goodness withdrawn from you or from me when we fail. St. Paul reminds us in his letter to the Church at Rome, *"But God proves his own love for us in that while we were still sinners, Christ died for us."* [Romans 5:8]

Whether we be sick or healthy, or even dying; when we have apparently outlived our usefulness to God and we no longer have strength to work in the church, visit the sick and lonely or even go to the polls to vote, God holds us, upholds us, as a mother holds and upholds her child.

Do you remember the parable of the *crazy* farmer who owned a vineyard? [Matthew 20:1-16] Then trust-it! The men hired by the farmer at the last hour of the day were loafers who, being lazy, hung around the unemployment agency during harvest time when farmers needed laborers. When they were finally hired, they did very little work. Yet, much to their dismay, they received a full day's pay for doing almost nothing.

The Rabbis told a similar parable, but in that parable, the reward was in proportion to the toil. The laborer who performed best on the job received the greatest reward. Jesus turned the whole business around and in doing so, not only left us with a radical critique of our Protestant work ethic which lies at the heart of our free enterprise system, but He also left us with a powerful image of the love of God. After all, no business can stay in business very long, no matter how profitable the trade, if the CEO gives full wages to those who do minimal work. That is irrational. And that is precisely the point! By human standards, the love of God for us is irrational, insane, mad, lunatic.

Divine love comes from a 'gracious God' at the very heart of things who is hopelessly in love with us . . . regardless of our indifference! That is who God is. That is what makes our lives significant, regardless of how we try to trivialize them. And that is the love we are bound to represent to others. "O give thanks to the Lord, for He is good; for His steadfast love endures forever."

Second, the Goodness of God is evidenced by the fact that both the Old Testament and the New Testament illustrate God's special love for the poor and the oppressed, the lonely and the afraid, the sick and the dying.

It would take a rewriting of the Scripture to substantiate the claim that the God of those Hebrew slaves-who invested Himself in a common laborer's Son as the One who heals diseases, frees the captives and sets at liberty people who are oppressed, is a God whose special love is only for the rich and powerful, the wellborn and the well-placed. *God loves us **all**,* I do believe. But anyone who reads the Bible will soon see a God who has a special love—if not bias—for those of us who suffer. That is the goodness of God.

Third, the Goodness of God is evidenced by the fact that God's love is active, not passive, energetic as well as emotive, and will never be withdrawn! Many had believed in God before, and some even understood something of the great goodness of God prior to that time. But the early Hebrew insight into God's ways and works (which they called the Covenant) was absolutely unique in its depth and scope, and later fulfillment in Jesus Christ.

The early Hebrews saw God as One who had entered into a relationship of communication and action with people, in which God promised to be their God and claimed them as His people. They perceived that God had committed Himself to them and passionately loved them with a determination they called "steadfast love." Every time you see these words in the Bible, you can be sure that the author has in mind God's Covenant and determination to hang with these on-again, off-again people. They understood their history, and the meaning of their individual lives, in terms of this love affair entered into by the Lord of the universe with His people. They sensed that all of life was a dialogue with the steadfast love of God that would never be taken from them.

When they were in bondage in Egypt, God delivered them. Why? No one knows, save that His steadfast love endures forever.

When they wandered for forty years in the wilderness, He protected them. That's hard to understand apart from the steadfast love that endures forever.

When they sinned, God was displeased and had every reason to forsake them for another people . . . but did not, for His steadfast love endures forever.

Then, in the fullness of time, many were given faith to see God's creative mind and recreating power made flesh in Jesus of Nazareth. They said to one another, "Rejoice, the Lord is at hand . . . " for His steadfast love endures forever.

When sin did its worst to erase Him from the pages of history, God did His best and raised Jesus from the dead . . . for His steadfast love endures forever. And when the earth beyond that little Fertile Crescent had been sufficiently prepared "by that Crazy Farmer" to receive its King, God gave the great commission and called forth the Church and sent it into all the world . . . for His steadfast love endures forever.

Sometimes I say to you that being Christian is not easy, and you know what I mean. Being Christian means believing that Jesus was right. And believing that Jesus was right means sharing in His experience of a God who really loves you and then living as one caught up in so great a love affair. Sometimes that is not easy, for it always requires one to put one's life, or one's need, or one's pain—into the hands of the Lord.

But sometimes I think I need to say to you: look, friend of mine, being Christian is really not very hard—especially for people whose time, strength and options in life seem to be running out—people who desperately need a Savior and a Friend. Then, being Christian is very easy. It all comes down to trusting in the trustworthiness of God. It is entrusting one's life and the lives of those you love into the strong hands of the One who made you, who loves you with the steadfast love that will never let you go. You may trip, but never out of His reach to catch. You will finally fall, if not in life, then surely in death. But I do honestly believe that you will fall no further than into His everlasting arms for eternal life.

Karl Barth, in his last visit to the United States, was asked by a student at the University of Chicago Divinity School, "What is the meaning of the Gospel?" The great Swiss theologian, who might have responded with theological equations or deep philosophical judgments, said very simply, "I learned the answer to that question at my mother's knee. 'Jesus loves me, this I know, for the Bible tells me so.'" Would it not be very bad if it were somehow otherwise? "O give thanks unto the Lord for He is good; His steadfast love endures forever."

During those forty days following the Resurrection Jesus made numerous appearances that are recorded in the New Testament. He mysteriously appeared and then, just as mysteriously, disappeared. There is a legend that originated in the second Century. The story says that Peter, the disciples, and the women (who were the last at the cross and the first at the tomb) gave a party for the risen Lord the night before the Ascension. Jesus, once again in his native Galilee, suddenly disappeared from the group. As the legend goes, Simon Peter went in search of the Lord and discovered Him walking alone by the Sea of Galilee. He approached Jesus and said, "Lord, this is our last evening together. Is something wrong?" And the Master responded to the big fisherman saying, "I was looking for Judas!"

"O give thanks to the Lord for He is good; His steadfast love endures forever." Amen.

Shouting Lips, Shallow Commitment!

> *"Hosanna! to the
> Son of David!"*
> John 12:13

I had seen the word before but quite frankly it had never grabbed my interest. One day I encountered it again and headed straight for the dictionary. The word: *oxymoron*. Mr. Webster says it is a figure of speech consisting of a combination of contradictory words and incongruous thoughts.

It suddenly hit me that oxymorons are found throughout our society. Some examples: Our market advertises *jumbo shrimp;* a well known furniture store in its ad this week has a sale on *authentic reproductions*; at O'Hare Airport yesterday I saw another one: *down escalator!* We very frequently use oxymorons in our speech.

Down South if we saw someone whom God had failed to touch with fine facial features, we called them *pretty ugly*. As I think about it, that could even be a *cruel kindness*.

And, of course, all of us who belong to this church are oxymorons because we call ourselves *United* Methodists. That was made more classical for me once when a Free Methodist Bishop commented: "You Methodists are about as *united* as we are *free*." About the only thing three Methodists can agree upon is what a fourth Methodist ought to give.

Today Christians throughout the world are celebrating Palm Sunday. In a sense 'Palm Sunday' is an oxymoron. Not that the words 'Palm' and 'Sunday' are contradictory, but the very day itself and what was taking place was a combination of contradictory words and actions and incongruous thoughts.

We often think of Palm Sunday as a 'parade' and as a rule parades conjure up thoughts of excitement. What is essential in this parade, however, is to realize that the point of view of the folks along the parade route was different from the point of view of Jesus as He entered the city.

The people who lined the roadway saw the coming of Jesus as a great promise for an even greater future but from the eyes of Jesus, it would be the start of the longest, saddest and most difficult week of his life.

The people crowding the streets were excited. They saw in Jesus a King or a warrior who would restore law and order. But from Jesus' vantage point, he was riding through the gates of hell. He was entering the worst possible place, under the meanest of circumstances at the greatest disadvantage.

The people had gathered there by the thousands. Normally, Jerusalem was a city of about 40,000 people. During Passover, we are told, the population swelled to over 200,000.

Thousands had heard of the 'rabbi' from Galilee and, like the crowds who turn out for the President, they sang their day's *'Hail To The Chief'*, a rendition which the Gospels report as *'Hosanna In The Highest!'* Yet Jesus must be feeling the pain of isolation and the threat of imminent death.

The people lining the roadway were excited about the possibilities of strength and security. The one riding the donkey, however, was talking about servanthood and sacrifice.

Palm Sunday was the ultimate of oxymorons. It was a combination of contradictory words and incongruous thoughts. What the people were waiting and looking for was something entirely different from what Jesus wanted to do and to accomplish.

In 1976 when Jimmy Carter and Gerald Ford were locked in a political battle for the Presidency, perhaps the most unusual candidate seeking an elected office in America was an independent who ran for *Mayor* of Bloomington, Indiana. His name was Leon Varjian, an Armenian who was a graduate math student at the University of Indiana. He wore a clown suit, carried a toy pistol, and wore a roll of masking tape on his wrist "because you never know when you might need some masking tape!" He had wonderful campaign promises. For one thing, Leon wanted to turn Bloomington into 'Fun City.' He wanted to turn the town square into a giant monopoly board and to convert the campus of the University into a giant amusement park. He wanted to make the University buildings into a Tomorrow-Land and a Yesterday-Land and wanted to put academic robes on Mickey Mouse and Bugs Bunny who would roam the campus.

The candidate promised that the Police would be given only plastic guns that would shoot corks. The fire department would give rides to children on Saturday afternoons. "We won't have to worry about fires interrupting the rides because we'll make fires illegal on Saturday afternoons." He also promised to carpet all the sidewalks and to make them 'one-way' so that people would not bump into each other. Well, Mr. Varjian was not elected but he did get some great publicity. He was a clown, of course, and his campaign was a spoof.

Does it bother you that Jesus was often looked upon as a clown? He must have looked that way to the religious leaders, Roman officials, and the proper people of Jerusalem that day. Somewhat clown-like,

Shouting Lips, Shallow Commitment

Jesus riding in such majesty on a donkey. How absurd! Like the candidate for mayor in Indiana, Jesus came to Jerusalem with a platform that seemed almost as absurd.

The triumphal entry of Jesus into Jerusalem was scheduled at the Feast of the Passover. It was a time when thousands of Jews descended on the Holy City. Jesus didn't time his entrance because he knew there would be a lot of people, but rather, so it could coincide with that historical event.

A thousand years or so earlier, the children of Israel were held in captivity in Egypt. They were unable to find freedom so that they could return to their homeland. God devised a plan of afflicting the Egyptians so that His Hebrew children could escape to the Promised Land. God sent Samuel, his death angel, who would swoop down over Egypt bringing as many as twelve plagues to the Egyptians.

God warned Moses to instruct the people to kill a lamb, sprinkle its blood on the doorpost and the angel would then pass over the Hebrew children and they would be spared. Jesus rode into Jerusalem, and, he reminded his fellow Jews of the time they were held in bondage and because of God, they were now free.

That is one of the reasons the church places such great emphasis on Palm Sunday. He comes into our midst once again, delivering us from whatever holds us in bondage. My fear is some people completely miss the significance of this Palm Sunday celebration. The reason is simply because Palm Sunday is an oxymoron.

Jesus came in weakness yet conquered as none had conquered before. Jesus came not with power . . . not on some white charger, a conquering hero, but in love, and the history-changing effects cannot to this day be fully measured. Jesus came to die at the hands of evil persons, yet in dying he triumphed over death. Jesus came to establish a kingdom . . . the Kingdom of God, and in so doing to set people free. This is the Palm Sunday oxymoron. But people with shouting lips and shallow commitment never sorted this out.

Jesus made it clear he didn't come to destroy the law but to fulfill it. He came so that we might have life and have it abundantly. In other words, Jesus brought a new way of looking at life.

Often what Jesus offered was an oxymoron. Someone wanted to know what they had to do to inherit eternal life. Jesus told them to go and sell all they had, give it to the poor, and follow him.

For all of us, that is an oxymoron. To be quite brutally genteel (if I may use that oxymoron) in 45 years in the ministry, I have yet to meet a layperson or a pastor who would be willing to sell all they had, give it to the poor, and follow Jesus.

It's a contradiction of thoughts. Somebody asked Jesus how they could save their life and Jesus replied, "by giving yourselves away," only then can we truly save our life. What an incongruous thought. And yet that is the genius of the Christian faith. We are to spend ourselves and empty ourselves.

One of my favorite newspaper columnists was Erma Bombeck. Since her death, I miss reading her down-to-earth, homespun wisdom and commentary on everyday life. Someone asked her once if she saved ideas, spread them out, so she'd have at least one strong column a week. I loved her response:

> I don't save anything. My pockets are empty at the end of a week. So is my refrigerator. So is my gas tank. So is my file of ideas. I trot out my best and next week I bargain with the Almighty, whimper, make promises for just three more columns in exchange for cleaning my oven.
>
> I didn't get to this point overnight. I came from a family of savers who were sired by poverty, raised in the Depression, and worshiped at the altar of self denial. Throughout the years, I've seen a fair number of my family who have died leaving candles that have never been lit, appliances that never got out of a box, and new sofas shrouded in chenille bedspreads.
>
> I had a relative who, for years, entertained in her basement. I once described the decor as 'Early Hot Water Heater.' We sat on glider swings and drank from plastic as we surveyed the room around us: a workbench, outdoor tables, mismatched lamps and stationary tubs. Upstairs was a perfectly beautiful living room that was mis-named.
>
> I always had a dream that when I am asked to give an account of my life to a higher court, it will go: 'So empty your pockets. What have you got left of your life? Any dreams unfulfilled? Any unused talent we gave you when you were born that you still have left? Any unsaid compliments or bits of love that you haven't spread around'? And I will answer, "I've nothing to return. I spent everything you gave me."

Erma's in the league with the man whose family gathered with the lawyer following his death and the lawyer read his will, "Being of sound mind I spent it all while I was alive . . ."

Following the reopening of China to the West, an American minister visited a group of Chinese and wanted to know how converts were won during the Communist occupation and cultural revolution. Some talked about the miracles, Jesus walking on water, turning water into wine, healing, calming storms. But one Christian said it was the hearing of the story of the Upper Room, how on the night before Christ died, Christ wrapped a towel around his waist and stooped to wash the feet of his disciples in complete humility. Said the Chinese Christian, "Such a thing we had never seen in any religion . . . that is when we

Shouting Lips, Shallow Commitment

knew that we in my house must follow Jesus."

That first Palm Sunday was an oxymoron. Many who shouted that day were looking for someone to provide security. That's not what Jesus had it mind. He offered another way. He took a towel. He emptied himself. He became a servant.

There is a play, whose title escapes me (that's what happens to folks over age 60). It's about a Jewish Zealot named Baruch who wants to return to law and order by military might. The people believe Jesus can accomplish this. In the drama there is a secret rendezvous dealing with two animals, a colt and a war-horse saddled and ready. Jesus is to signal his intentions by which animal he chooses. **Jesus chooses the colt.**

It occurred to me that you could almost sum up the entire Gospel story with those four words: Jesus chose the colt.

In other words Jesus rejected what people meant by kingship. He would rule all right, but from a colt. He would reign, all right, but from a cross. He would be a king, all right, but as a shepherd, not as a golden-crowned male monarch.

Palm Sunday was truly an oxymoron. The people were anticipating great joy and excitement. On that same day, at that same parade, Jesus was anticipating suffering and death. I recently discovered that the word *pain* comes from Greek antiquity. It means *penalty*. Most folks try to avoid pain. We spend multi-millions of dollars each year attempting to convince ourselves that the best painkiller is Advil, Bayer, Bufferin or Tylenol.

The Bible places a higher priority on pain. While it readily admits that some pain results from not obeying God, it also shows that some pain, suffering and discomfort, can be the direct consequence of faithfulness. Perhaps Jesus could have avoided a lot of pain by simply avoiding Jerusalem, but He did not. He came as a shepherd, caring and willing to sacrifice all for His sheep. It was not suicidal, but sacrificial.

Every once in a while someone catches the full meaning of what Jesus was attempting to do. Whenever that happens, there is great joy . . . especially to a preacher.

"Good News From A Graveyard"

Now upon the first day of the week, very early in the morning, they came unto the sepulchre, bringing the spices which they had prepared, and certain others with them. And they found the stone rolled away from the sepulchre. And they entered in, and found not the body of the Lord Jesus. And it came to pass, as they were much perplexed thereabout, behold, two men stood by them in shining garments: And as they were afraid, and bowed down their faces to the earth, they said unto them, Why seek ye the living among the dead? He is not here, but is risen:"

Text: St. Luke 24:1-12

The burnished dream ended in a bloody nightmare on Friday. The splendid hope was now a mangled despair. The clouds had been dark over Calvary on that Friday afternoon but now the setting sun illuminated a hill shaped like a human skull. Two men, dressed in the garments that suggested both wealth and prominence tenderly lowered a blood-stained body from a Roman cross and wrapped it in a linen winding sheet. They began, then, the difficult descent to a garden at the foot of a rocky path. They paused before a new and opened tomb—uttered a prayer—and hastily placed the body in the tomb. They dared not tarry for the sun was on the horizon and with the sunset came the Sabbath when no Jew could touch the dead. The voice of the Galilean was silenced and his body was gently laid in a borrowed tomb.

Jesus was the great borrower of history. He borrowed a stable stall to be born in; he borrowed a boat to preach from; he borrowed a donkey to ride into Jerusalem; he borrowed an upper room in which to eat the Passover supper; and last of all, he had to borrow Joseph of Arimathea's tomb to be buried in.

Evening fell quietly over the garden of Joseph of Arimathea and a Roman guard paced back and forth before the tomb—now closed by a heavy stone at its door. Then it was dark. The bats came from their haunts and screeched to one another. A lonely jackal lifted his head to the first evening star and howled to a nameless mate. In the City of Jerusalem discouraged men hid themselves in fear and despair, muttering to themselves, "We had thought it would be He who would redeem Israel."

The Jewish Sabbath passed. No Jew entered the garden or molested the tomb. Pilate had doubled the guard and sealed the tomb with the stamp of Imperial Rome. He would have no resurrection nonsense to plague his kingdom or his sleep. Enough was enough and

Good News From A Graveyard

he wanted no more of the Nazarene. As for the Nazarene's disciples—well, three years before the Master had called them to become fishers of men. Now that his flame had died away they would once more become fishers of fish. Their King crucified like a criminal. Their Messiah ended up—not on a throne, but on a cross—hailed as King on Sunday . . . dead like a common thief on Friday. They were the remaining survivors of a broken cause—stumbling blindly down the hill their eyes filled with tears they could not stop. They were utterly crushed—beaten—disappointed. As for those Apostles, Jesus was dead and that was that.

Who are these men walking along the street in Jerusalem with heads bowed? Oh yes, Peter and James and John. Why don't they speak? Why are they so downcast?

'Peter, what's the matter?'
'Jesus is dead.'
'James, why so dejected?'
'Jesus is dead.'
'John, why are you so hopeless?'
'Jesus is dead.'

That's the Good Friday answer and that's why they were without hope and without purpose.

'Peter, where are you going?'
'I go a'fishing.'
'James and John, where are you going?'
'We're going back to mending nets.'

See, that's where they were going—back to their old jobs. That's what the disciples had decided to do. Leave Jerusalem and take up their old work.

What else was there left to do? Go back to the old familiar boats in Galilee with their unpadded seats and patched sails. Back to the mending of their nets—sadder—but wiser men! The past three years with Him had been a sentimental interlude which had ended, and the Apostles were quite ready to pick up their lives where they had left off at the Master's call. Their Master and friend had been put to death and they were through.

Then came Sunday morning!

The first rays of the early morning sun cast a great light that caused the dew drops on the flowers to sparkle like diamonds. It was the same garden—yet strangely different. The atmosphere of the garden had changed.

In the Bible there are written four *Lives* of Christ. We know them as the four *Gospels*. Four historians within the faith soberly reported that he died and was duly buried. But, *"On the third day, He rose*

again...!" **That is the Easter message!**
That is the Good News From A Graveyard!

We may talk about springtime and new life, flowers and the greening of the good earth, Easter eggs and bunny rabbits—myths and symbols—but that is not the Easter proclamation.

Easter rests on one particular story, a quite specific drama about a man (not a myth) who was ordered crucified by Pontius Pilate (a man of history) and who was reported to have risen from the grave.

Since that first Easter His followers have defied all reason to proclaim that the Jew of Nazareth was the Son of God, who, by dying for human sin, reconciled the world to its Creator and Sustainer. Christianity has always been content to stand or fall by this paradox, this mystery, this unfathomable truth.

"If Christ had not been raised," wrote St. Paul to the young church at Corinth, *"then our preaching is in vain, and your faith is in vain. If Christ has not been raised, your faith is futile and you are still in your sins."*

No event in the New Testament is better attested than the Resurrection of Jesus of Nazareth from the dead. Not only is it reported in overwhelming detail in the Gospels but it is affirmed in twenty-three of the twenty-seven New Testament books.

It is the reason that Easter has been—and is—the crowning Festival Day of the Christian Year for twenty centuries. It is the reason our churches are crowded on Easter Sunday.

A chapter of history began that day which continues to this very day. History was turned into HIS-story. The subject is God, not man; and only God can know the full truth of this historic event. Our only road to understanding of this divine history is through faith—faith in the reality and truth of what the Evangelists so incoherently described.

Karl Barth, the Swiss theologian, would ask, *"Do you want to believe in the living Christ? We may believe in Him only if we believe in his bodily resurrection. This is the content of the New Testament. We are always free to reject it, but not to modify it, nor to pretend that the New Testament tells something else. We may accept or refuse the message, but we may not change it."*

There is no mumbling or misgiving in the New Testament about the Resurrection. *"Now is Christ risen from the dead. Who can separate us from the love of God... not life, not death, not anything. Now are we the sons and daughters of God and it does not yet appear what we shall be."*

Luke tells us that women came to the tomb of Joseph of Arimathea, not in hope but in despair. In the agony of their grief, they feel the need to do something. There was precious little they could do.

They had been last at the cross. Now they are the first at the tomb.

"Now it was Mary Magdalene and Joanna and Mary, the mother of James and the other women with them . . ." Luke says. Mary, whose sins had been forgiven, could not do much. Jesus was dead and discredited. But she loved her Lord and simply wanted to be there. Surely, Mary, the mother of our Lord was there. To their utter amazement when they arrived at the tomb, it was empty.

They are asked, *"Why are you looking for him who is alive among the dead? He is not here; He is risen."* They hasten swiftly to tell the eleven that Jesus had risen from the dead.

Were they greeted by a shout of joy that the miracle their Lord had foretold had really happened? Not at all. There they sat, the gloomy, bewildered disciples, puzzled that the One whom they had believed to be God's Messiah had been crucified and was dead. The story of his coming to life again and of the women's vision at the tomb *". . . seemed to them as idle tales, and they believed them not."* What is the record afterwards?

Take another look at these Apostles only three days after the crucifixion and what a change we see in them!

"Peter, why are you so glad?"

"Jesus lives!"

"James, why so jubilant?"

"Jesus is alive!"

"John, why have you not gone back to your old job?"

"Jesus lives!"

You see a complete change in their hearts and minds. We may not be able to understand the story of the empty tomb but you simply can't argue away or account for the extraordinary change in the disciples without saying that in their experience they learned that Jesus was not dead but was alive.

Jesus was not dead; he was gloriously alive. He would be with them always and under the spell of His living spirit, eleven disillusioned and defeated men were transformed into men of power. They marched out into their world with heads erect and eyes alight to be more than conquerors in the Master's name.

Eleven men were lifted out of despair to new heights of joy and commitment. After the Resurrection cowards found some backbone and were changed into fearless heroes. Dwarfs became giants! The Resurrection of Christ made Christianity into a worldwide faith. His resurrection message became the cornerstone of the Christian Church.

That crowded hour of Easter dawn has been called the watershed of history. In that baffling hour of Resurrection, God invaded human history to affirm the endless sovereignty of Christ through time and tide. In one staggering event, God snatched from human hands the victory won by naked power and set the goal of human striving in the high calling of Christian discipleship. There, in the garden of Joseph of Arimathea, God laid the touchstone of human progress by which events and movements are measured. St. John says God affirmed, "... in Him was life and the life was the light of men."

We can't escape the fact that progress is no more than meaningless motion unless it is movement toward the mind of Christ. Every step we take from birth to death has a relationship to the living Christ; every event of history stands in judgment before Him.

Over and over again in history, God confronts us with the imperative: *"This is my beloved Son, in whom I am well pleased. Hear ye him!"* [Mark 1:11]

There have been many crowded hours of destiny along the corridors of time—along each and everyone's own personal *yellow-brick road*. There have been many occasions where the past has been sucked into the present to change 'the shape of things to come.' There have been times when eternity has been poured into one hour. Now and then something new and decisive enters our personal history and whether we wish to or not, we have to reckon with it. There comes an hour when newness crowds our lives with shattering impact. Always, however, when the event occurs, it stands in judgment before Jesus Christ.

Life came to the world like a shining light in the Garden but history also speaks of death coming like a shroud at the hands of Caesar and Genghis Kahn, Napoleon and Bismarck, Hitler and Mussolini, Khruschev and Mao Tse Tung, to mention but a few. The question before the human race today is not a question of Christ or chaos. We have chaos in the closing years of this millennium. It is rather a question of Christ or final catastrophe.

We are again outside that tomb on Easter morn standing in judgment of the Resurrection. *"In Him was life and the life was the light of men"* [John 1: 4] and we will have to choose.

Too many of us approach life and our day-to-day activity with the question, *"What's in it for me?"* The trouble lies in the fact that we are asking the wrong question. The real question is, *"What's in it that lasts?"*

God made it clear that first Easter dawn that Christ-in-us is all there is that lasts—that death cannot touch. Hell is a condition, a condition of character in which there is nothing that lasts. Heaven is a condition wherein the mind and spirit of Christ has come to dwell in us.

That is what Oscar Wilde tried to say in his story of the sinner standing in the judgment hall before God. God says, with a touch of sadness: *"I'll have you sent to hell."* The answer comes back from the depths of pain: *"You can't! I'm there already."* There is silence, then God speaks again: *"I'll send you to heaven."* The answer comes once more: *"You can't—I've never been able to imagine it."*

You cannot imagine heaven unless you've known and cherished things death cannot touch. William James, the famed psychologist, once expressed it this way, *"The best argument I know for an immortal life is the existence of a person who deserves one."* You cannot imagine heaven if life is filled with shoddy things inside—with nothing on our mind but the question, *"What's in it for me."* Every hour is crowded with life or death for in every hour we are making decisive choices. We choose between love that lasts and lust that dies; between truth that stands forever and lies that flounder; between goodness that is permanent and evil that is transient. Life crowds us now, pressing us to make our choice.

The crowning note of Easter is a note of triumph and hope. In the Resurrection, the love of God invaded history. With the eloquence of an empty tomb, God offered his redeeming love to us. Though we crucify Him day by day, his love remains as steady as the stars. He comes to us in our crowded hours of choice, waiting with endless patience for us to answer with our lives.

Sometimes I wonder how many of us are *good* in God's eyes. The best of us are, at times, blundering fools—selfish, stubborn and belligerent. We are so busy feathering our own nests we don't really care about the Kingdom of God except perhaps at Christmas or Easter. Someone asked George Bernard Shaw which person would he pick among the great men and women on the earth to start a new dispensation if he could be Noah in another flood. The old playwright flashed back, *"I'd let 'em all drown."* Well, maybe Shaw would, but God would not. God keeps loving with a patience beyond anything we know. Now and then we take His hand, perhaps in tears, and find a crowded wonderful hour of life that marks our turning and our redemption. Once in a hundred years there is a St. Francis, a Martin Luther, a John Wesley, a Ghandi, a Schweitzer, a Mother Teresa, who answers the love of God with such devotion that history is altered and, at least for a while, a new path is charted.

Not only the great and well-known are examples of this Resurrection faith, but also large numbers of unknown and unrecognized souls who may leave no memorials behind them, but people, who by their kindnesses and sacrifices and faithfulness have sustained all of life.

What kind of business do we think God is in anyway? Is He like the artist who shows up at the State Fair every year or the ethnic festivals at Hart Plaza, who draws in colored chalks the portraits of people? For fifteen dollars he draws an excellent likeness. Sometimes the rain comes, the chalk likeness is ruined and the disappointed people throw them down to be trampled under the feet of the pedestrians.

Do you think that's the kind of business God is in? Do you think He brings human souls into being, gives them minds to think with and hearts to love with and hands to work with and then lets the rain and the feet of time wash them away as if they had no value at all? That's incredible.

"Someday," said Dwight L. Moody, *"someday, you'll read in the newspapers that Dwight L. Moody of Northfield is dead. Don't you believe a word of it. At that moment I shall be more alive than I am now."*

We need, dear friends, to recover the power of the Resurrection story. Our world hungers for that story to penetrate our doubts and fears.

One of my favorite preachers, the late Dr. Ralph Sockman of Christ Church in New York City, wrote: *"The foundation of my belief in eternal life reaches farther back than the Resurrection of Christ. It rests on the very integrity of the universe. This belief in life beyond the grave has persisted through all races, and this conviction is strongest in our healthiest moments and rises out of our noblest emotion, that of love.*

"The Creator has endowed us with power to love, to believe, to hope. These powers are as deep in our nature as the hungers of the body for food and drink and air. Surely the Creator who keeps faith with the appetites of our bodies will not play false with the hungers of our souls."

The hope of life beyond death is universal but let's face the fact that the hope is always mixed with fear. And the Resurrection marks the victory of that hope over that fear.

He is alive! We serve a Risen Savior, He's in the world today! He lives! You ask me how I know He lives? He lives within my heart!

The good news of Easter? There is victory of life over death, of goodness over evil, of hope over fear! Thanks be to God, who gives us the victory through our Lord, Jesus Christ.

"Four Critical Questions: Four Frank Answers"

". . . And he who earns wages, earns wages to put them into a bag with holes . . ."
Haggai 1:6e

". . . What shall I return to the LORD for all his bounty to me?"
Ps. 116:12

". . . Just then there came a man named Jairus, a leader of the synagogue. He fell at Jesus' feet and begged him to come to his house, for he had an only daughter, about twelve years old, who was dying. As he went, the crowds pressed in on him. . . . While he was still speaking, someone came from the leader's house to say, "Your daughter is dead; do not trouble the teacher any longer." When Jesus heard this, he replied, "Do not fear. Only believe, and she will be saved." When he came to the house, he did not allow anyone to enter with him, except Peter, John, and James, and the child's father and mother. They were all weeping and wailing for her; but he said, "Do not weep; for she is not dead but sleeping." And they laughed at him, knowing that she was dead. But he took her by the hand and called out, "Child, get up!" Her spirit returned, and she got up at once. Then he directed them to give her something to eat. Her parents were astounded; but he ordered them to tell no one what had happened."
Luke 8:41-42, 49-56

The pioneer Methodist Circuit Riders used to say that four books are necessary to propagate the Gospel: *the 'Good Book'*—the Bible; *the 'Church Book'*—our Methodist manual, *The Discipline*; *the 'Hymn Book'*; *and the 'Pocket' Book*. This is a sermon about the latter but rather than talk about the *pocketbook* I want to speak of stewardship.

Whenever a matter of giving and spending money comes up, there are almost invariably four crucial questions which rise up in our minds and demand an answer. Today is Stewardship Sunday—commitment day—when we are called to focus on our responsibility to God and His Church and to make an intentional response. It is a good time now to give our attention to those questions.

The first question almost always is: *"How much does it cost?"* In this stewardship crusade you will help determine what it will cost. No budget has been brought to you by a pastor or a Finance Committee or Administrative Council. No budget has been set. There are no figures to agree or disagree on. Following your commitment and that of your brothers and sisters in this congregation that question will be answered.

I am asking you to do what Paul asked the first century Church to do. *"First of all, they gave themselves to the Lord . . . "* [2 Cor 8:5b] That is the first cost. If whatever we are willing to give does not begin with the gift of oneself, it doesn't represent the deepest and the best within us and it is not really much of a gift at all. Jesus told a story about a widow who came into the synagogue, opened up her purse and gave away the very last penny she had. It's the story of the *Widow's Mite*. She not only gave, she sacrificed. We need to remember that she opened up her heart before she opened up her purse. We *possess*, but God *owns*. It matters not how little or how much we have, the only question is, *"Have we been faithful to God in the use of what we have?"* Everything that we have—ability, money, skill, talents—belongs to God and we will ultimately be judged by how we use it.

Let me share with you a modern parable: *"Once upon a time there was a man who had nothing. God gave him ten apples: the first three to eat, the second three to trade for shelter, the third three to swap for clothing and the last apple so that he might have something to give back to God in gratitude for the other nine? What happened? The man ate the first three apples, traded the second three for shelter and swapped the third three for clothing. But he looked at the tenth apple and knew it should be returned to God. But this apple looked bigger and juicier than all the rest. Reasoning that God had all the other apples in the world, the man ate the tenth apple and gave the core back to God."*

There is no portion of our time that is *our* time, and the rest, *God's;* there is no part of money that is *our* money and the rest, *God's* money. It is all His; He made it all—gives it all—and He has simply trusted it to us for His service.

The second question which is apt to come up is, **"Have we got the money?"** We are in a period of high income and employment in our state and nation. In fact, things have not been this good in forty years. Years ago a five or six percent income on a security was considered a pretty good return; for the past three years we have experienced in America a phenomenal stock market where investors have averaged over 20% annually from their portfolios. Not only is unemployment down but so is inflation. The real concern, according to the second most powerful man in the nation, Mr. Alan Greenspan, may be 'deflation' instead of 'inflation'.

Many of us have resources which we often forget. In banking circles the term *"dead money"* is used to describe the forgotten money on deposit in national banks. You would think that people who deposit money in the bank would remember it, but this is not the case. An article came out in our newspapers in the Summer of 1997 that citizens of Michigan had millions of dollars of *"dead money"*. They even listed columns and columns of names, by cities, to try to find the rightful owners.

In a Christian view of life, there is another kind of *"dead money"*: money that we have that is not needed for everyday living but which neither is invested for the good of humanity.. This is *"dead money"* and it is something to cry about. How many times in your life and mine has a need been presented and an opportunity to respond given, but we made no response because our assets are in a *"dead money"* account? How often have we taken what God has given us and buried it in selfish pursuits?

I heard once of a church having a stewardship crusade much like yours. In making calls upon those who did not come on Stewardship Sunday, one of the volunteers ran into a touchy family who expressed their indignation at the continuing request for money. *"We are always being asked for money. I'm sick and tired of it. The Church never calls on us unless they want money"* or so the caller was told. The dear volunteer responded, *"Well, let me tell you a true story. A little boy was born in my home many years ago. From the day of his birth, he cost me money and every year he cost more. At first there was just food and clothing and medicine. As he grew he wanted a bike and I had to buy him one. Even public school cost money. And when he went to college he cost me a whole lot more money. In his senior year in college he was taken very sick. Doctor's bills and hospital bills piled up. Then they stopped. My son had died and do you know my friend,"* he concluded, *"that son hasn't cost me a cent, not a red cent since."* I leave the application to you.

I'm completing 24 years at Metropolitan as Senior Pastor and 45 years in the ministry. It breaks my heart when I ride by the buildings that consecrated Christians built and later generations allowed to slip away. The congregations that lost them were not the ones that built those churches. In most instances they were handed down from previous generations. But isn't that true of all or most of our churches? How many people in your Church were here when it was organized? The church is a gift to us.

Whenever I enter the walls of any place of sacred worship, I am haunted by all of those who have gone before. I think of the Church as a gift out of the Catacombs of Rome and the deserts of Israel. The Church was a legacy to us over the centuries by the sacrifice of believers and the sobbing of the saints who have gone before. Wherever a congregation meets and by whatever name it calls itself, there are crosses on her walls, blood on the lintels of her doors and bones beneath every altar in Christendom. Our generation may call it *our church,* and rightly so, but it is a gift outright.

One of the saddest days I've spent in Detroit the last 25 years was on Woodward Avenue. I was a part of a crowd that lined up on Woodward to go inside a church. It was a church which helped build a hospital for the famous Burma surgeon. It was the church where a former mayor of Detroit, Mayor Pingree, worshipped. It was a church at one time with 3,000 members, a church where three-times Presidential candidate, William Jennings Bryan, came and preached to throngs. Once again crowds were lining up to go into that church—the Woodward Avenue Baptist Church. What for? To worship and hear a noted preacher? No. A music concert and the thrill of a great pipe organ? No! They were going to a sale. The church had closed its doors and everything was now up for sale. Dishes were sold for ten cents and a quarter. Grand pianos were sold for a few hundred dollars. Bronze plaques were being bought for $2.50. Chairs—for a dollar. Tiffany stained-glass windows were sold for a song. I went to the sale after having read an article in the Detroit Free Press which headlined, *"Members Let Church Die."* I wept. I thought of the consecrated laymen and lay women who sacrificed to build it. I thought of the people who came to Christ, were baptized, married and worshipped there. I also thought of those who deserted her when times got tough and I thought of a Pastor who felt the church should *'die with dignity'*. I thought of all those things—that day and then later—when it burned to the ground.

Personally, I want the cause of Christ and the witness of the Christian faith to be alive and grow, not only on Woodward Avenue but everywhere. I'd like to see more churches and stronger congregations and fewer dance halls and bar rooms.

So, the second question, *"Have we got the money?"* is really *"Can we afford to do in this church what Christ is calling us to do?"* In fact, for my part, I doubt if we can really afford anything else.

The third crucial question to be asked, whenever the matter of stewardship is discussed and money is to be raised and spent, is this: **"Can I get the same thing cheaper somewhere else?"**

We all look for bargains, good buys, and there is no virtue in spending more than we have to. If you can buy an item cheaper at K-Mart than at some other business, go for it. That's the spirit of the marketplace.

When Ulysses S. Grant was a boy of eight he wanted badly to buy a pony from a neighbor and he asked his father for the $25 asking price. His father agreed, Grant said years later, but tried to educate him in the ways of the world. He told him the animal was probably worth only $20 and he should offer that amount. If it was not accepted he was to offer $22.50 and if that didn't close the deal he could spend the entire $25. When the young Grant got to the neighbors, he blurted out in one sentence, *"Papa says I may offer you $20, but if you won't take it, I'm to offer $22.50, and if you won't take that, I can give you $25."*

There may not be many horse traders in this congregation, but not many of us need to be told how much he spent.

Can we get what we want cheaper. In one sense I suppose we could; no one has to belong to a church or give a dollar in any way to the cause of Christ. One could live and raise a family and die on a completely secular and self-centered basis, or at the most with a few fees for occasional professional services.

But, and I am ashamed almost to say it, I doubt if many get their religion as cheaply as United Methodists. That is true of us as a generation. With our national income at an all time high we actually give a smaller percentage of it to philanthropic and benevolent causes than we did in the worst years of the Depression.

That's true of us as a denomination. Year after year United Methodists are near the bottom in the list for *per capita* giving in American churches. A pastor told me some years back of a professional woman baptized and brought up Catholic who married a Methodist husband. In the premarital counseling they told the pastor they would be giving separately to the Church and she asked how much she ought to give. Not wishing to emphasize money too much, the Methodist preacher, in an easygoing Protestant fashion said, *"Oh, you decide that for yourself."* Like a shot from a gun came her reaction, *"Well, all I've got to say is it may be a lot cheaper to be a Methodist than to be a Catholic."* Could we get our religion cheaper? I suppose so. But I hardly know where.

Finally, the most crucial question of all when money is being raised and spent is this: *"Will whatever we are buying give satisfaction?"* Will it be a good buy over the long run? Or, is it just flash merchandise which will soon disappoint?

I read from an obscure prophet in the Old Testament named Haggai. He lived in an era of severe economic readjustment and inflation. He was trying to raise the money for major needs—the rebuilding of the Jewish Temple which had been leveled to the ground by invaders. He was not just a superficial realist but a genuine one and he pointed out that people *". . . were sowing much but reaping little—they drank but were still thirsty—clothed themselves but were still cold and he who earns wages, earns wages to put them into a bag with holes."*

Which is to say that there are a lot of things in life that are okay as far as they go, but they just don't go far enough. There's nothing particularly wrong with them, but they don't have any lasting value. Food, clothes, entertainment, automobiles, are all in this category and I am not suggesting that they should be ignored because they are needed in our modern life. Yet, they are transitory.

But the wise person will not give them a monopoly on time and attention. The prudent does not labor for them and for them alone. Because, if one does, one finds out sooner or later that they are a bag with holes. If we are wise we try to find something of lasting, or even better, increasing value. It was the wisest man of all who told his friends not to lay up treasures that thieves could break in and steal, or rust and disintegration destroy, but to lay up treasures that last forever.

If you try to buy bodily health and vigor, worthy as these are, the years will steal them from you. Remember there are folk all around us who spend their health to earn their wealth and then, the wealth to try to regain their health. And, one day they lose it all. If you try to buy luxury and self-indulgence, you are increasingly at the mercy of thieves and insurance men (there *is* a difference), not to mention—fickle fashion.

But suppose your real treasure is spiritual. Suppose you handle money in such a way as to produce noble character in yourself and others. Not even death can take that from you.

Suppose your aim is to do God's will with what you have. Can anyone or anything stop you? Suppose you put your money into transforming lives and churches and Christian camps and mission work and old folks homes. Can anything or anyone, ever take away the satisfaction? On the contrary, the longer you watch that money at work and the more you know about it, the greater will be your joy.

I read this morning the story of Jairus from the Gospels. That story reminds me that a generation or so ago there was a novel called, *The Daughter of Jairus*, based on the biblical story.

The novel tells how Jairus, proud and rich, blurted out extravagant promises of giving Jesus half his property if He would only heal his daughter. When the girl recovered though, he began to have second thoughts. He said to himself that the strain and anxiety had made him impetuous and he had overreacted. So he went to Jesus to try to wriggle out of his bargain. He pointed out that he had been in an agitated frame of mind and besides, the girl hadn't really been as sick as she seemed, or she couldn't have been cured so quickly.

Jesus made no answer. So, Jairus went on, somewhat louder, to say that of course he meant to give Jesus something—perhaps three fat sheep, or a cask of wine, and a cask of olive oil. Still, no response.

Jairus' voice rose shrilly, *"And perhaps, I would be willing to throw in a couple of bags of silver!"*

To which Jesus replied quietly, *"There is nothing to pay."*

Jairus was stunned. *"Nothing?"*

"Nothing."

"I would like," Jesus said, *"to see the child again before I leave."*

I have been speaking here as though we were buying something when we support the cause of Christ or make an intention to give as though there was something to pay. There is not, of course. There is never anything to pay for the salvation He gives and for the healing touch of the Great Physician.. But there is everything to give.

Perhaps the question you are called to give answer to today is not, *"How much shall I give?"* The real question is, *"How much will I keep?"* And as you struggle to answer that question, I remind you—

everything you own
will one day
belong
to someone else!